Books by Erin McHugh:

WHO?

WHAT?

WHERE?

WHEN?

WHY?

WHO?

Erin McHugh

Sterling Publishing Co., Inc.
New York

Library of Congress Cataloging-in-Publication Data Available

10 9 8 7 6 5 4 3 2 1

Published by Sterling Publishing Co., Inc.
387 Park Avenue South, New York, NY 10016

Distributed in Canada by Sterling Publishing
c/o Canadian Manda Group, 165 Dufferin Street
Toronto, Ontario, Canada M6K 3H6
Distributed in Great Britain by Chrysalis Books Group PLC
The Chrysalis Building, Bramley Road, London W10 6SP, England
Distributed in Australia by Capricorn Link (Australia) Pty. Ltd.
P.O. Box 704, Windsor, NSW 2756, Australia

Manufactured in the United States of America

Sterling ISBN 1-4027-2569-8

For information about custom editions, special sales, premium and corporate purchases, please contact Sterling Special Sales Department at 800-805-5489 or specialsales@sterlingpub.com.

WHO?

HURRICAN'TS

Hurricanes So Damaging Their Names Have Been Retired

Name	*Last Heard from*	*Name*	*Last Heard From*
Agnes	1972	Elena	1985
Alicia	1983	Eloise	1975
Allen	1980	Flora	1963
Andrew	1992	Frederic	1979
Anita	1977	Gilbert	1988
Audrey	1957	Gloria	1985
Betsy	1965	Hattie	1961
Beulah	1967	Hazel	1954
Bob	1991	Hilda	1964
Camille	1969	Hugo	1989
Carla	1961	Ione	1955
Carmen	1974	Inez	1966
Carol	1954	Janet	1955
Celia	1970	Joan	1988
Cleo	1964	Klaus	1990
Connie	1955	Luis	1995
David	1979	Marilyn	1995
Diana	1990	Mitch	1998
Diane	1955	Opal	1995
Donna	1960	Roxanne	1995
Dora	1964		

YAWN

Famous Insomniacs

Caligula * Joseph Conrad * Marlene Dietrich * Alexandre Dumas * W. C. Fields * F. Scott Fitzgerald * Galileo * Hermann Goering * Rudyard Kipling * Alexander Pope

BLACK PATENT

Curiously, free blacks were allowed to hold U.S. patents, even before the Civil War. Often craftspeople and machinists, African Americans have held some of our most important patents.

Thomas Jennings was the first black man to hold a U.S. patent, which was granted in 1821 for a dry-cleaning process. He spent most of his considerable earnings promoting abolitionist causes.

Henry Blair received a patent in 1834 for his corn-planting machine. Two years later, he invented a corn-harvesting machine as well.

Norbert Rillieux patented an evaporator for refining sugar in 1845 that is still in use.

Elijah McCoy patented a device for lubricating steam engines in 1872, which was the first of fifty-seven patents issued to him in his lifetime.

Lewis Howard Latimer was granted a patent for an electric lamp in 1881 and a carbon light bulb filament in 1882. He was the only black man working in Thomas Edison's lab.

Sarah E. Goode designed a folding cabinet bed, which was patented in 1885, making her the first black woman granted a U.S. patent.

Anna M. Mangin patented a pastry fork in 1892.

Madame C. J. Walker patented a hair-care system for black men and women in the early 1900s, sales of which made her the wealthiest black woman in America. She donated most of her fortune to black charities.

Garrett Augustus Morgan patented a gas mask in 1914, which was widely used in World War I. He went on to design automated traffic lights that were awarded patents in 1923.

George Washington Carver was granted three patents in his lifetime, all issued in 1927 for a processing system he invented for producing paints and stains from the humble soybean. Today, Carver is most widely known for inventing more than three hundred uses for the peanut.

Frederick McKinley Jones patented a refrigeration system in 1938 that revolutionized long-haul trucking. A specialist in refrigeration, Jones gathered more than forty patents in his lifetime.

David Crosthwaite patented a heating system that he went on to install in New York's Radio City Music Hall. Crosthwaite earned more than forty patents in his lifetime for advancements made in heating, ventilating, and air-conditioning systems.

Granville T. Woods held more than sixty patents, his most important for a system that made telegraph communication between two traveling trains possible.

TRIPLE CROWN WINNERS

Horse	*Year*
Sir Barton	1919
Gallant Fox	1930
Omaha	1935
War Admiral	1937
Whirlaway	1941
Count Fleet	1943
Assault	1946
Citation	1948
Secretariat	1973
Seattle Slew	1977
Affirmed	1978

ALL-TIME GREAT CONEY ISLAND SIDESHOW STARS

Baby Dee the Human Hermaphrodite
Bambi the Mermaid
Christine Hell the Fire Eater
Eak the Geek, the Illustrated Man
Helen Melon ("She needs four men to hug her and a boxcar to lug her")
Indestructible Indio
Koko the Killer Clown
Ravi the Scorpion Mystic
The Twisted Shockmeister
Ula the Painproof Rubber Girl
Zenobia the Bearded Lady

INVENTORS AND THEIR FAMOUS—AND LESS FAMOUS—INVENTIONS

Inventor	*Famous Invention*	*Less Famous Invention*
Isaac Newton	Laws of gravity (1684)	Reflecting telescope (1668)
Eli Whitney	Cotton gin (1794)	Mass production (1798)
Benjamin Franklin	Lightning conductor (1752)	Bifocal lens (1784)
Robert Fulton	Long-distance steamboat (1807)	Metal-clad submarine (1800)
Samuel F. B. Morse	Morse code (1838)	Underwater telegraph cable (1842)
Alfred Nobel	Dynamite (1867)	Nitroglycerine (1865)
Thomas Alva Edison	Incandescent light bulb (1879)	Mimeograph (1875) and alkaline battery (1900)

ELVIS!

In 1993, the U.S. Postal Service issued a commemorative stamp featuring a portrait of the "King." The most popular stamp ever, more than 124 million have been collected by philatelists since its release. The next bestselling celebrity commemoratives are Marilyn Monroe, which sold 46.3 million stamps (number 6 overall) followed by Bugs Bunny, which sold 45.3 million (number 7 overall).

WHO AM I?

Our Human Ancestors

Who?	*How Old?*	*Profile*
Ardipithecus ramidus kadabba	5.8–5.2 million years ago	Walked upright; 4 feet tall
Ardipithecus ramidus ramidus	c. 4.4 million years	Similar to *A. ramidus kadabba*
Australopithecus anamensis	c. 4.2 million years	Walked upright; possible ancestor of Lucy
Australopithecus afarensis	c. 3.2 million years	Lucy; 3.5 feet tall; lived in family groups in Africa
Australopithecus africanus	c. 2.5 million years	Descendant of Lucy
Australopithecus robustus	c. 2 million years	Related to *A. africanus*
Homo habilis	c. 2 million years	Brain enlarged; used simple tools
Homo erectus	c. 1.8 million years	Java Man; used fire; lived in caves; pre–*Homo sapiens*
Homo sapiens idaltu	160,000 years (?)	Anatomically modern human
Homo sapiens sapiens	100,000 years (?)	Anatomically modern human

The World's Most Famous Eight-Man Baseball Club

THE "WHO'S ON FIRST?" TEAM

Abbott and Costello's Shtick from The Naughty Nineties

Who:	First base
What:	Second base
I Don't Know:	Third base
Why:	Left field
Because:	Center field
Tomorrow:	Pitcher
Today:	Catcher
I Don't Give a Darn:	Shortstop

There is no right fielder mentioned in the skit.

WHO WILL HELP?

The 2000 U.S. census points out the heartening statistic that 40 to 50 percent of adults between the ages of thirty-five and forty-four do some volunteer work. Though they are in one of life's busiest times in terms of both family and career, this is also the age group with the highest volunteer percentage. The volunteers in this age group are nearly equally divided between men and women.

THE EDSEL, the longest-running joke in the car industry—and one of its biggest flops—was not built by Edsel Ford but named for him after his death in 1943. Edsel himself was an automobile maker of extraordinary vision and distinction and was the man responsible for the design of the Lincoln Continental Mark I, which debuted in 1939.

QUESTIONABLE KUDOS: NOT-SO-GREAT FIRSTS FOR WOMEN

Goodwife (Goody) Wright was the first woman wrongly accused of witchcraft in America, in 1622.

Goodwife Norman and **Mary Hammon** were the first women arrested and tried for lesbianism, in the Massachusetts Bay Colony in 1649. In an odd judicial decision, Goody Norman was sentenced to "public acknowledgment," while Ms. Hammon was acquitted.

Alice Thomas, in 1670s Boston, was the country's first female tavern keeper and, haplessly, the first to be arrested—for selling liquor without a license, profaning the Sabbath, receiving stolen goods, and "frequent secret and unseasonable entertainment in her house to Lewd Lascivious and Notorious persons of both sexes, giving them opportunity to commit Carnale Wickedness."

Mary (Molly) Brandt was the first woman found spying against the United States by informing the British of Patriot movements in New York State, in 1777.

Lucy Stone was the first woman arrested on charges of civil disobedience, in 1858, for protesting taxation without representation. Stone was also the first married woman to retain her maiden name.

Lucy Ware Webb Hayes became the first First Lady to ban liquor in the White House, earning her the nickname

"Lemonade Lucy," in 1877. Hayes was also the first woman to enroll at Ohio Wesleyan University.

Sally Tomkins was the first commissioned officer in the Confederate Army, in 1861.

Edith Eleanor McLean was the first premature baby placed in an incubator, then called a "hatching cradle," at Ward's Island in New York City, in 1888. She weighed 2 pounds, 7 ounces.

Evylyn Thomas was the first automobile accident victim, in 1896. She was riding her bicycle in New York City.

Sarah Emma Edmonds was the first woman inducted into the Grand Army of the Republic, an organization of Civil War veterans, in 1897. In 1861, the New Brunswick, Canada, native enlisted in Michigan as Franklin Thompson. Edmonds became a spy ("disguising" herself as a woman), deserted the army, and finally returned as a nurse.

Anna Edson Taylor was the first woman to go over Niagara Falls alone in a barrel (4.5 feet by 3 feet), in 1901. Her feat brought her a cash prize, which she used to save her ranch from foreclosure.

Nan Jane Aspinall was the first woman to ride alone across the United States on horseback, in 1910. She covered 4,500 miles in 301 days, but seriously delayed delivery of the letter she carried from the mayor of San Francisco to the mayor of New York by riding less than half of the time.

Maude B. Campbell was the first paying woman customer on a commercial plane in 1926. Campbell purchased a round trip ticket for $180 and flew from Salt Lake City, Utah, to Los Angeles in an open cockpit biplane. The trip lasted nine hours each way and Ms. Campbell was required to wear a parachute.

Mary Babnick Brown was the first woman whose hair (brunette, 34 inches long) was used as crosshairs for World War II B-17 bombsights.

Roberta A. Kankus was the first woman licensed as a commercial nuclear power plant operator at the pastoral-sounding Peach Bottom Power Plant, in 1976.

Dorothy Dietrich was the first woman ever to catch a bullet in her mouth, at the International Brotherhood of Magicians Convention, in 1980. Many had already found this perilous trick fatal, and even Houdini himself refused to attempt it.

Judith A. Resnick and **Sharon Christa McAuliffe** were the first women to die on a space flight, in 1986, aboard the *Challenger*. Resnick was a career astronaut. McAuliffe was chosen by President Reagan because she was a teacher; she planned to give science lessons to children via the Public Broadcasting System during the flight.

Arlette Rafferty Schweitzer was the first woman to bear her own grandchildren, acting as her daughter's surrogate, in 1991.

BLANCHETTE is Little Red Riding Hood's given name.

FOUNDING FATHERS

Father of the United Nations	Cordell Hull (1871–1955), U.S. secretary of state
Father of the Blues	W. C. Handy (1873–1958), composer
Father of the Irish Republic	Eamon de Valera (1882–1975), president of Sinn Fein
Father of the Four-Letter Word	Henry Miller (1891–1980), author of *Tropic of Cancer*
Father of Country Music	Jimmie Rodgers (1897–1933), singer and guitarist
Father of the Gossip Column	Walter Winchell (1897–1972), U.S. journalist
Father of the Atomic Bomb	Dr. J. Robert Oppenheimer (1904–1967), physicist

THREE STOOGES—SIX NAMES

Moe Howard: Moses Horwitz
Larry Fine: Louis Feinberg
Curly Howard: Jerome Lester Horwitz
Shemp Howard: Samuel Horwitz
Joe Besser: Jerome Besser
Joe DeRita: Joseph Wardell

And yes, all three Horwitzes were brothers.

MULTIPLE PULITZER PRIZE WINNERS

	Four	
Eugene O'Neill	Drama	*Beyond the Horizon* (1920) *Anna Christie* (1922) *Strange Interlude* (1928) *Long Day's Journey into Night* (1957)
Robert E. Sherwood	Drama	*Idiot's Delight* (1936) *Abe Lincoln in Illinois* (1939) *There Shall Be No Night* (1941)
	Biography	*Roosevelt and Hopkins* (1949)

	Three	
Edward Albee	Drama	*A Delicate Balance* (1967) *Seascape* (1975) *Three Tall Women* (1994)
Herbert Block (HerBlock)	Editorial cartooning	NEA Service (1942) *Washington Post* and *Times-Herald* (1954) *Washington Post* (1979)
Paul Conrad	Editorial cartooning	Formerly of *Denver Post* (1964), later of *Los Angeles Times* (1971 and 1984)

Edmund Duffy	Editorial cartooning	*Baltimore Sun* (1931, 1934, and 1940)
Rollin Kirby	Editorial cartooning	*New York World* (1922, 1925, and 1929)
Jeffrey K. MacNelly	Editorial cartooning	*Richmond (VA) News-Leader* (1972 and 1978) *Chicago Tribune* (1985)
Thornton Wilder	Drama	*The Bridge of San Luis Rey* (1928), *Our Town* (1938), *The Skin of Our Teeth* (1943)

Two

William Faulkner	Fiction	*A Fable* (1955) *The Reivers* (1963)
Nelson Harding	Editorial cartooning	*Brooklyn Eagle* (1927 and 1928)
George S. Kaufman	Drama	*Of Thee I Sing* (with Morrie Ryskind and Ira Gershwin) (1932) *You Can't Take It with You* (with Moss Hart) (1937)
Bill Mauldin	Editorial cartooning	United Features Syndicate (1945) *St. Louis Post-Dispatch* (1959)
Vaughn Shoemaker	Editorial cartooning	*Chicago Daily News* (1938 and 1947)

Paul Szep	Editorial cartooning	*Boston Globe* (1974 and 1977)
Booth Tarkington	Fiction	*The Magnificent Ambersons* (1919) *Alice Adams* (1922)
Barbara W. Tuchman	Nonfiction	*The Guns of August* (1963) *Stilwell and the American Experience in China, 1911–1945* (1972)
Tennessee Williams	Drama	*A Streetcar Named Desire* (1948) *Cat on a Hot Tin Roof* (1955)
August Wilson	Drama	*Fences* (1987) *The Piano Lesson* (1990)

WHO IS "THE 12TH MAN"?

Originally, "The 12th Man" was a Texas A&M basketball player named E. King Gill, who was asked to hurriedly suit up for an ailing football team member back in 1922. Though Gill never saw any action, he became known as "The 12th Man," and his spirit lives on. Today, the entire Texas A&M student body acts as the 12th Man, and stands at the ready throughout the entire game whenever A&M plays at home. Official preseason tryouts are held for an annual 12th Man position on the bench as well.

50 GREATEST SCREEN LEGENDS

	Actors	*Actresses*
1.	Humphrey Bogart	Katharine Hepburn
2.	Cary Grant	Bette Davis
3.	James Stewart	Audrey Hepburn
4.	Marlon Brando	Ingrid Bergman
5.	Fred Astaire	Greta Garbo
6.	Henry Fonda	Marilyn Monroe
7.	Clark Gable	Elizabeth Taylor
8.	James Cagney	Judy Garland
9.	Spencer Tracy	Marlene Dietrich
10.	Charlie Chaplin	Joan Crawford
11.	Gary Cooper	Barbara Stanwyk
12.	Gregory Peck	Claudette Colbert
13.	John Wayne	Grace Kelly
14.	Lawrence Olivier	Ginger Rogers
15.	Gene Kelley	Mae West
16.	Orson Welles	Vivien Leigh
17.	Kirk Douglas	Lillian Gish
18.	James Dean	Shirley Temple
19.	Burt Lancaster	Rita Hayworth
20.	The Marx Brothers	Lauren Bacall
21.	Buster Keaton	Sophia Loren
22.	Sidney Poitier	Jean Harlow
23.	Robert Mitchum	Carole Lombard
24.	Edward G. Robinson	Mary Pickford
25.	William Holden	Ava Gardner

Source: American Film Institute, 2004.

THE WOMEN OF PLAYBOY

Famous Girls, Infamous Covers of the Twentieth Century

The Fifties

Marilyn Monroe (December 1953 and September 1955)
Jayne Mansfield (February 1956)
Zsa Zsa Gabor (March 1957)
Julie Newmar (May 1957)
Sophia Loren (September 1957)
Kim Novak (October 1959)

The Sixties

Elizabeth Taylor (January 1963)
Elke Somers (September 1964)
Ursula Andress (July 1965)
Jane Fonda (August 1966)
Ann-Margret (October 1966)
Joan Collins (March 1969)
Vanessa Redgrave (April 1969)

The Seventies

Melanie Griffith (October 1976)
Raquel Welch (February 1977)
Margaux Hemingway (June 1978)
Farrah Fawcett (December 1978)
Nastassia Kinski (August 1979)

The Eighties

Suzanne Somers (February 1980)
Crystal Gayle (November 1981)
Rae Dawn Chong (May 1982)
Mariel Hemingway (April 1982)
Kim Bassinger (February 1983)
Bridget Bardot (March 1985)
Madonna (September 1985)

Mamie Van Doren (February 1986)
Vanna White (July 1986)
Morgan Fairchild (August 1986)
Jessica Hahn (November 1987)
LaToya Jackson (March 1989)

The Nineties
Sharon Stone (July 1990)
Sherilyn Fenn (December 1990)*
Stephanie Seymour (March 1991)
Mimi Rogers (March 1993)
Elle Macpherson (May 1994)
Patti Davis (July 1994)
Robin Givens (September 1994)
Drew Barrymore (January 1995)
Nancy Sinatra (March 1995)
Cindy Crawford (July 1988 and October 1998)
Katarina Witt (December 1998)

*Sherilyn Fenn also enjoyed a career as a *Playboy* Bunny, along with other superchicks Lauren Hutton (1960), Gloria Steinem (1963), and Deborah Harry (1968).

WHO SHOT J. R.?

Kristin Shepard, J. R. Ewing's sister-in-law
on March 21, 1980 in *Dallas*, Texas

Since the game's invention in 1935, THE MONOPOLY GUY was known as Rich Uncle Moneybags. It was only with the millennium that he was renamed Mr. Monopoly.

HEAVENS ABOVE!

Patron Saints, the People They Protect, and Their Strange Symbols in Art

Patron Saint	*Who Is Protected*	*Symbols*
Agatha	Bellmakers, nurses	Tongs
Agnes of Rome	Girls	Lamb
Ambrose of Milan	Beekeepers	Bees
Anne	Canada, mothers	Door
Antony	Domestic animals	Hog
Augustine of Hippo	Printers	Pen
Barbara	Artillerymen	Cannon
Bartholomew the Apostle	Leathermakers	Tanner's knife
Benedict	Poison sufferers	Broken cup
Blais	Throat ailments	Wax candle
Catherine of Siena, Italy	Fire prevention	Stigmata
Cecelia	Musicians	Organ
Christopher	Bookbinders, travelers	Forest, giant
Cosmos and Damian	Druggists	Box of ointment
Dominic	Choirboys	Rosary
Elizabeth of Hungary	Bakers	Bread

Patron Saint	*Who Is Protected*	*Symbols*
Francis of Assisi	Animals	Birds, deer, fish
Francis Xavier	Emigrants and immigrants	Ship
Genevieve	Disasters, Paris	Keys
George	Soldiers	Dragon
Gregory the Great	Singers	Tiara
Hilary of Poitiers	Snake bite victims	Stick
Jerome	Librarian	Lion
John the Baptist	Lambs	Head on a platter
Lawrence	Cooks, France	Gridiron
Lucy of Syracuse	The blind	Eyes
Luke the Apostle	Artists	Palette
Margaret	Pregnant women	Dragon
Martha	Housewives, servants	Holy water sprinkler
Mary Magdalen	Penitent sinners	Alabaster box of ointment
Maurus	Gout sufferers	Crutch
Monica	Married women	Girdle and tears
Nicholas of Myra	Pawnbrokers	Three purses

Patron Saint	*Who Is Protected*	*Symbols*
Patrick	Engineers, Ireland	Harp and shamrock
Peter the Apostle	Fishermen	Rooster
Philip Neri	Rome	Altar
Roch	Dogs and dog lovers	Dog
Rose of Lima	Florists, the Americas	City
Sebastian	Archers, athletes	Arrows
Vincent de Paul	Charities, volunteers	Children
Vincent Ferrer	Builders	Captives

WHO GOES THERE?

Dr. Byron McKeeby and Nan Wood were the real folks who modeled in 1930 for Grant Woods's famous *American Gothic.* They were neither married nor farmers, being the dentist and sister of the artist. In fact, they never even sat together for the portrait.

KEEPING UP WITH THE JONESES

The Ten Most Common Surnames in the United States

Smith * Johnson * Williams * Jones * Brown * Davis * Miller * Wilson * Moore * Taylor

PEOPLE MAGAZINE'S SEXIEST MEN

Year	*Hunk*	*Age*
1985	Mel Gibson	29
1986	Mark Harmon	34
1987	Harry Hamlin	35
1988	John F. Kennedy Jr.	27
1989	Sean Connery	58
1990	Tom Cruise	27
1991	Patrick Swayze	38
1992	Nick Nolte	51
1995	Brad Pitt	31
1996	Denzel Washington	41
1997	George Clooney	35
1998	Harrison Ford	55
1999	Richard Gere	50
2000	Brad Pitt	36
2001	Pierce Brosnan	47
2002	Ben Affleck	29
2003	Johnny Depp	39
2004	Jude Law	32
2005	Brad Pitt	41

In 1848 in Seneca Falls, New York, the FIRST WOMEN'S RIGHTS CONVENTION met and drew up a Declaration of Sentiments, which was signed by sixty-eight women and thirty-two men.

WOODROW WILSON is the only president to ever hold a Ph.D. (Johns Hopkins, Political Science, 1886).

SATANIC MONIKERS

Better the Devil You Know . . .

Name	*Biblical Reference*
Abaddon	Revelation 9:11
The accuser of our brethren	Revelation 12:10
The adversary	1 Peter 5:8
Apollyon	Revelation 9:11
Beelzebub	Matthew 12:24; Mark 3:22; Luke 11:15
Belial	2 Corinthians 6:15
The Devil	Matthew 4:1
Dragon	Revelation 12:9 and 20:2
The enemy	Matthew 13:39
Father of all lies	John 8:44
God of this world	2 Corinthians 4:4
King of Babylon	Isaiah 14:4
King of Tyrus	Ezekiel 28:12
Little horn	Daniel 7:8
Lucifer	Isaiah 14:12
Man of sin	2 Thessalonians 2:3
That old serpent	Revelation 12:9 and 20:2

Name	*Biblical Reference*
Power of darkness	Colossians 1:13
Prince of the power of the air	Ephesians 2:2
Prince that shall come	Daniel 9:26
Prince of Tyrus	Ezekiel 28:2
Prince of this world	John 12:31
Ruler of the darkness of this world	Ephesians 6:12
Satan	Job 1:6
Serpent	Genesis 3:1
Son of perdition	John 17:12
The tempter	Matthew 4:3
The wicked one	Matthew 13:19

WORLD'S GREATEST CALLING CARD

MISS HOLLY GOLIGHTLY TRAVELLING

Hats off to *Breakfast at Tiffany's* . . .

PINOCCHIO means "pine-eye" in Italian.

NEWFANGLED PROBLEMS, NEW PATRON SAINTS

Some Actual Modern-Day Assignments of the Catholic Church

Patron of	*Saint*
Advertisers and advertising	St. Bernardine of Siena, known for the power of his sermons
Aircraft pilots and crew	The Virgin Mary; her Assumption into heaven shows her ascending through the clouds
Flight attendants	St. Bona of Pisa, famous pilgrim
Astronauts	St. Joseph of Cupertino, chosen for his ability to levitate
Motorists	St. Frances of Rome, as her continuous vision of her guardian angel enabled her to see at night
Telecommunications	St. Gabriel the Archangel (the word archangel means "chief messenger")
Highways	John the Baptist, who wrote "Make straight the way of the Lord" (John 1:23)
Scientists	St. Albertus Magnus, a Dominican priest and scientist considered to be the equal of Aristotle in his time

NUMBER, PLEASE

What Your Social Security Number Means . . .

AREA NUMBERS

The first three numbers originally represented the state in which a person first applied for a social security number. Since 1973, the Social Security Administration has assigned numbers and issued cards based on the zip code.

GROUP NUMBERS

The two middle digits, which range from 01 to 99, are simply used to break all the social security numbers with the same area number into smaller blocks.

SERIAL NUMBERS

The last four serial numbers are randomly generated and run consecutively from 0001 through 9999, subdividing each middle group of numbers.

GOT A CLUE?

Anyone who played the board game Clue as a kid remembers the names of the playing pieces and their attendant colors:

Mr. Green	green
Colonel Mustard	yellow
Mrs. Peacock	blue
Professor Plum	purple
Miss Scarlet	red
Mrs. White	white

. . . but less well known is the name of the victim: Mr. Boddy.

WITCHCRAFT, WICKED WITCHCRAFT

Lady Alice Kyteler (1280–?) was a wealthy Irish woman accused of witchcraft by her fourth husband and his family, who all believed she had lured him into marrying her for his money. Soon, the children of her former husbands accused her of hastening their fathers' deaths, leaving them impoverished. Her alleged transgressions ranged from heresy to nocturnal meetings with the devil himself (in the form of a large black dog). A servant claimed Lady Alice had taught her to become a witch, and that they flew through the air on a broomstick. Kyteler eventually escaped to England, banished, and disappeared from sight.

Joan of Navarre (1370–1437), the wife of King Henry IV of England, was accused in 1419 of being a witch and of conspiracy to depose the king. She was later pardoned and reinstated as queen in 1422.

Anne Boleyn (1507–1536), second wife of King Henry VIII, was claimed to be a witch when she was unable to bear him a son. That she had a sixth finger (or more likely a vestigial sixth nail, the mark of a witch) on one hand didn't help. Boleyn was executed on patently false charges of witchcraft, incest, and adultery.

Elisabeth Sawyer (?–1621), upon being condemned to death, confessed her "long and close-carried witchery." The devil, she said, came to her and assisted her in the injuries she inflicted. Mother Sawyer confessed that she had plagued her neighbors' cattle and caused the death of two infants. She was hanged, and shortly thereafter a famous play, *The Witch of Edmonton*, was written.

Margaret Jones (?–1648), a Massachusetts Bay Colony physician, became the first woman accused of being a witch to be executed, when patients under her care got sicker instead of well. (It turned out that many of her patients simply weren't taking their medicine.) She was hanged in 1648.

Mother Shipton (most likely Ursula Sonthiel, 1488–1561) was a fifteenth-century Yorkshire woman and England's most famous witch. She was said to have powers of healing and spell-casting; she set forth many prophecies about modern times, scientific inventions, new technology, wars, and politics, which were later interpreted as having come true, from the Great Fire of London in 1666 to the advent of modern technology, and even her own death in 1561.

The Mother Shipton Prophecies

The fiery year as soon as O'er,
Peace shall then be as before;
Plenty everywhere be found,
And men with swords shall plough the ground.
The time shall come when seas of blood
Shall mingle with a greater flood.
Carriages without horses shall go.
And accidents fill the world with woe.

Around the world thoughts shall fly
In the twinkling of an eye.

Waters shall yet more wonders do,
How strange yet shall be true.
The world upside down shall be,

And gold found at the root of a tree.
Through hills men shall ride
And no horse or ass be by their side;
Under water men shall walk,
Shall ride, shall sleep, shall talk;
In the air men shall be seen,
In white, in black, and in green.

Iron in the water shall float
As easy as a wooden boat;
Gold shall be found, and found
In a land that's not now known.
Fire and water shall more wonders do
England shall at last admit a Jew;
The Jew that was held in scorn
Shall of a Christian be then born.

A house of glass shall come to pass
In England, but alas!
War will follow with the work
In the land of the Pagan and Turk
And state and state in fierce strife
Will seek each other's life
But when the North shall divide the South
An eagle shall build in the lion's mouth.

An Ape shall appear in a Leap year
That shall put all womankind in fear
And Adam's make shall be disputed
And Roman faith shall like rooted,
And England will turn around.
Thunder shall shake the earth;
Lightning shall rend asunder;

Water shall fill the earth;
Fire shall do its work.

Three times shall lovely France
Be led to dance a bloody dance;
Before her people shall be free.
Three tyrant rulers shall she see;
Three times the People rule alone;
Three times the People's hope is gone;
Three rulers in succession see,
Each spring from different dynasty.
Then shall the worser fight be done,
England and France shall be as one.

Waters shall flow where corn shall grow
Corn shall grow where waters doth flow
Houses shall appear in the vales below
And covered by hail and snow;
White shall be black then turn grey
And a fair Lady be married thrice.

All England's sons that plough the land
Shall be seen, book in hand;
Learning shall so ebb and flow,
The poor shall most wisdom know.

NO LOVE

Frederick Louis, eldest son of George II, quarrelled bitterly with his father and led the political opposition to the king. The feud ended when Frederick died in 1751 as a result of being struck by a tennis ball.

OOH, BABY, BABY

The Most Popular Names for Children in the Year 1900 . . .

1.	John	Mary
2.	William	Helen
3.	James	Anna
4.	George	Margaret
5.	Charles	Ruth
6.	Joseph	Elizabeth
7.	Frank	Marie
8.	Henry	Rose
9.	Robert	Florence
10.	Harry	Bertha

*And Today** . . .

1.	Jacob	Emily
2.	Michael	Emma
3.	Joshua	Madison
4.	Matthew	Olivia
5.	Ethan	Hannah
6.	Andrew	Abigail
7.	Daniel	Isabella
8.	William	Ashley
9.	Joseph	Samantha
10.	Christopher	Elizabeth

*2004, according to the Social Security Administration

WILLIAM KEMMLER was the first American criminal to be executed, in Auburn, New York, on August 6, 1890.

DOG TAGS DECODED

November 1941 to July 1943

First line	First name of soldier, second initial, surname	CLARENCE R JONES
Second line	Army serial number Tetanus immunization Tetanus	37337566 T42 43 O
Third line	Name of next of kin	FRED JONES
Fourth line	Street address of next of kin	2843 FEDERAL PL
Fifth line	city and state; religion	DENVER COLO P

Current Version

First line	Last name
Second line	First name, middle initial
Third line	Social Security number
Fourth line	Blood Type
Fifth line	Religion

Though U.S. presidents have never been known to be a musical bunch, "COOL CAL" COOLIDGE apparently played a pretty mean harmonica.

"THE HOLLYWOOD TEN"

This famous—or infamous—group was blacklisted from the movie industry for refusing to testify about communism in Hollywood in 1947 before the House Un-American Activities Committee. They were convicted of contempt of Congress and served prison sentences. Their futures were checkered.

Alvah Bessie (1904–1985) worked as a stage manager in San Francisco, then turned to novel writing.

Herbert Biberman (1900–1971) financed his own work, including the 1954 movie *Salt of the Earth* with Adrian Scott, which was not allowed to be shown in the United States until 1965.

Lester Cole (1904–1985), fired from writing *Viva Zapata!* in 1952, penned his work under an assumed name for the rest of his life, including the screenplay for the extremely popular *Born Free* in 1965.

Edward Dmytryk (1908–1999), after reconsidering, reappeared before HUAC in 1951 and named names. This change of heart resulted in a future in directing; one of his films was *The Caine Mutiny*.

Ring Lardner Jr. (1915–2000), sacked by Fox, worked under a pseudonym until the blacklist lifted, and won an Oscar in 1970 for Best Original Screenplay for *M*A*S*H*.

John Howard Lawson (1894–1977), blacklisted by all the studios, moved to Mexico and wrote Marxist interpretations of drama and filmmaking until his death.

Albert Maltz (1908–1985) wrote without credit for *The Robe* in 1953, and, in the 1970s, worked on other less successful movies under his own name.

Samuel Ornitz (1890–1957) spent the rest of his life as a novelist; one of his titles was the bestselling *Bride of the Sabbath,* in 1951.

Adrian Scott (1912–1973), blacklisted for twenty-one years, wrote under a pseudonym for television. He sued RKO Studios for wrongful dismissal; his case was finally thrown out by the Supreme Court in 1957.

Dalton Trumbo (1905–1976) was the first blacklisted writer to resume using his own name in 1960, with *Spartacus.* He wrote screenplays for several popular movies until his death.

WE KNEW THEM WHEN

What They Were Called Before They Became Big

Radiohead	On a Friday
The Beach Boys	Carl and the Passions
Procul Harem	The Paramounts
Talking Heads	The Artistics
The Byrds	The Beefeaters
The Who	The High Numbers
Depeche Mode	Composition of Sound
Blondie	The Stilettos
Black Sabbath	Earth

ANIMAL HOUSES

Animal	*Male*	*Female*	*Young*
Ass	Jack	Jenny	Foal
Bear	Boar	Sow	Cub
Cat	Tom	Queen	Kitten
Cattle	Bull	Cow	Calf
Chicken	Rooster	Hen	Chick
Deer	Buck	Doe	Fawn
Dog	Dog	Bitch	Pup
Duck	Drake	Duck	Duckling
Elephant	Bull	Cow	Calf
Fox	Dog	Vixen	Cub
Goose	Gander	Goose	Gosling
Horse	Stallion	Mare	Foal
Lion	Lion	Lioness	Cub
Sheep	Ram	Ewe	Lamb
Swan	Cob	Pen	Cygnet
Swine	Boar	Sow	Piglet
Tiger	Tiger	Tigress	Cub
Whale	Bull	Cow	Calf
Wolf	Dog	Bitch	Pup

BILLBOARD'S #1 RECORD RECORDS

Artist: The Beatles—20
Writer: Paul McCartney—32
Producer: George Martin—23
Label: Columbia—92

THE POCAHONTAS EXCEPTION

Pocahontas (1595–1617) is an early American heroine born Matoaka, daughter of Powhatan, an Indian chief, but from childhood she was known as Pocahontas. She made her first mark on history when she helped save the fledgling colony of Jamestown, Virginia, from extinction by supplying its new residents with food, at which time she befriended founding colonist John Smith.

Pocahontas married Englishman John Rolfe, who took her to England, where she became the toast of high society, including English royalty. She contracted smallpox while in England, however, and died there. Many years later, her only son, Thomas, sailed back to Virginia, claimed his grandfather's land, and killed or enslaved many of his mother's Indian relatives.

Regardless of Thomas's feelings, his parents had wed with the approval of Virginia's governor, and because Pocahontas was of royal (albeit aborigine) blood, the statutes in Virginia made an exception in their case at a time when interracial marriages were prohibited. The Virginia Colony's racist laws stated that virtually any black or Native American blood made a "white" person black or Native American; however, there was a colonial statutory Pocahontas Exception for the English descendants of Rolfe and Pocahontas, which in 1924 was reenacted by the U.S. Virginia State legislature. The Pocahontas Exception remained on the books in Virginia until overturned in the Supreme Court decision *Loving v. Virginia* in 1967. Today, white descendants of the Native American heroine often list her with pride atop their family tree.

POPEYE 'N' PALS

Popeye	Salty sailorman and love of Olive Oyl
Poopdeck Pappy	Popeye's dad, imprisoned on Goon Island
Peepeye, Pipeye, Poopeye, and Pupeye	Popeye's rambunctious quadruplet nephews
Olive Oyl	Anorexic, high-strung, girlfriend of Popeye
Swee' Pea	Snugglie-clad baby left on the doorstep and adopted by Popeye, who called him his "adoptid orphink"
Castor Oyl	Olive's brother
Cole and Nana Oyl	Olive and Castor's dad and mom
Ham Gravy	Pre-Popeye boyfriend of Olive Oyl
Bluto	Muscle-bound and determined bully who's out to deck Popeye and steal Olive Oyl
Brutus	Later Bluto lookalike
Alice the Goon	Flowerpot-hatted, near-mute giantess whose perpetual mission was to kidnap Popeye and spirit him away to Goon Island
Eugene the Jeep	mischievous pup given as a birthday gift to Popeye from Olive Oyl

J. Wellington Wimpy	Popeye's penny-pinching, hamburger-craving mooch of a best friend, known to his friends simply as Wimpy
Sea Hag	longtime stalker and archenemy
Toar	Sea Hag's flunkie, now Popeye ally
George G. Geezil	Shoe cobbler and Wimpy's nemesis
Rough House	Chef/owner of Rough House's Café

TENNIS RULES FOR BLACK BOYS

Arthur Ashe said that as a youth, a black player followed unwritten rules playing tennis against white kids:

- Engage—never enrage—white opponents
- When in doubt, call your opponent's ball in
- Before changing court sides, pick up your opponent's balls and hand them to him
- Always make sure your behavior is beyond reproach

CINDY LOU WHO: Literature's most famous Who, and one of the Who-ville Whos; melted the heart of the Grinch in Dr. Seuss's holiday tale *How the Grinch Stole Christmas.*

The NEW YORK YANKEES have been honored seven times in a New York City tickertape parade, the most ever.

WHO YOU CALLIN' MOB?

The Very Best Mafia Nicknames

Louis "Pretty" Amberg (1897–1935)	Independent racketeer and killer
Otto "Abbadabba" Berman (1880–1935)	Policy game fixer
Ruggerio "Richie the Boot" Boiardo (1891–1984)	New Jersey Mafia patriarch
Joseph "Joe Bananas" Bonanno (1905–2002)	New York "Big 5" family boss
Ralph "Bottles" Capone (1893–1974)	Al's brother and Chicago overlord
Vincent "Mad Dog" Coll (1909–1932)	Quintessential Irish 1930s gangster
William "Willie Potatoes" Daddano (1925–1975)	Chicago outfit torturer
Jack "Legs" Diamond (1896–1931)	Lone-wolf racketeer
Sam "Momo" Giancana (1908–1975)	Most powerful boss west of New York
Sam "Golf Bag" Hunt (?–1956)	Capone hit man
Ellsworth "Bumpy" Johnson (1906–1968)	Black mafioso from Harlem
Alvin "Creepy" Karpis (1907–1979)	Public Enemy wooed by Mafia

Joseph "Socks" Lanza (1904–1968)	Genovese captain and fish industry boss
Thomas "Three-Finger Brown" Lucchese (1900–1967)	"Five Families" Don
Peter "The Clutching Hand" Morello (1870–1930)	Took over Black Hand with brothers
Samuel J. "Nails" Morton (?–1924)	Jewish Chicago mobster
Abe "Kid Twist" Reles (1907–1941)	Murder, Inc. hit man
Paul "The Waiter" Ricca (1897–1972)	Top Chicago outfit man
Jacob "Gurrah" Shapiro (1900–1947)	Murder, Inc. right-hand man

. . . And If You Wonder Why They Call Them Animals:

Anthony "Tony Ducks" Corallo (1913–2000)	Lucchese boss
Sammy "The Bull" Gravano (1945–)	John Gotti's underboss
Murray Llewellyn "The Camel" Humphries (1899–1972)	Chicago chieftain
Matthew "Matty the Horse" Ianniello (1920–?)	Genovese capo and porn czar
George "Bugs" Moran (1893–1957)	Chicago Prohibition gangster

Ignazio "Lupo the Wolf" Mafia Saietta (1877–1947)	Organized New York City activity
Benjamin "Bugsy" Siegal (1906–1947)	Gangster and Las Vegas developer
Tony "The Ant" Spilotro (1938–1986)	Vegas mobster; model for Joe Pesci character in *Casino*
Angelo "Quack-Quack" Ruggiero (?–1986)	Talkative Gotti capo
Jimmy "The Weasel" Fratianno (1913–1993)	Mobster-turned-informant
Philip "Chicken Man" Testa (1924–1981)	Philadelphia underboss

"THEY'RE GIVIN' YOU A NUMBER, AND TAKIN' AWAY YOUR NAME"

Types of Secret Agent Men

Agent: A person, usually foreign, who obtains information for an intelligence organization.

Notional agent: A nonexistent agent created by an intelligence agency to deceive the enemy.

Secret agent: An undercover agent or anyone acting as a clandestine spy or saboteur for an intelligence operation.

Agent of influence: A person whose job is to wield opinion in important places. Agents of influence are usually politicians, academics, journalists, scientists, and the like.

Agent provocateur: An agent who provokes illegal rioting, rebellion, mutiny, treason, or sabotage by those under suspicion, making them liable to punishment.

Bagman: An agent who handles the money, either by acting as paymaster to spies, or by handing out bribes to those in authority.

Counterspy: An agent who works with a counterintelligence agency to expose or squelch a spy's ability to obtain information, usually by leaking disinformation.

Courier: An agent who retrieves and/or delivers messages, documents, and so on, usually with no idea of informational content.

Defector-in-place: An agent who has defected, but remains in his previous position in order to act as a double agent.

Defector: A spy who voluntarily changes sides.

Double agent: A spy who works for both sides, but who is loyal to only one; in other words, a spy who is employed by the enemy and performs a real service for them, while reporting valuable information back to his original agency.

ANGEL HIERARCHY

Seraphim
Cherubim
Thrones
Dominions
Virtues
Powers
Principalities
Archangels
Angels

WHO'S ON THE MONEY

The Faces of U.S. Currency

Since the U.S. government started issuing currency in 1861, bills and gold certificates have been printed in denominations from $1 to $100,000. Today, only the $1, $2, $5, $10, $20, $50, and $100 Federal Reserve Notes are printed. Bills in the denominations of $500 and $1,000 may still be found in circulation, and there are approximately two hundred $5,000 and three hundred $10,000 bills out there, though most of them are with collectors. The $100,000 bill was primarily used in intragovernment transactions between banks, but the advent of electronic transfers has made its use all but obsolete.

Only three of the denominations have not pictured U.S. presidents: these three show the first secretary of the treasury (Alexander Hamilton), a statesman and inventor (Benjamin Franklin), and the creator of the national banking system (Salmon P. Chase).

$1	George Washington	$100	Benjamin Franklin
$2	Thomas Jefferson	$500	William McKinley
$5	Abraham Lincoln	$1,000	Grover Cleveland
$10	Alexander Hamilton	$5,000	James Madison
$20	Andrew Jackson	$10,000	Salmon P. Chase
$50	Ulysses S. Grant	$100,000	Woodrow Wilson

By 1792, Congress was intent on establishing a coin system for the new country. The Coinage Act authorized the Mint and prescribed the standards, with the smallest denomination the half cent—soon known as the "little sister"—which was first struck in July 1793, just four months after the one-cent coin. Since then, several denominations have been minted:

1792	Half disme (½ dime), and cent	1796	Quarter dollar
1794	Half dollar	1850	$20 double eagle
1794	Silver dollar	1851	3 Cent
1795	$5 Half eagle	1854	$3
1795	$10 Eagle	1864	2 Cent
1796	Dime	1866	Nickel
		1875	20 Cent

CURRENT U.S. COINAGE

One cent	Abraham Lincoln	Half dollar	John F. Kennedy
Nickel	Thomas Jefferson	Silver dollar	Susan B. Anthony
Dime	Franklin D. Roosevelt	Golden dollar	Sacagawea
Quarter dollar	George Washington		

SHORT-LIVED

Arguably the two biggest jobs on earth have each had one incredibly short-term occupant. Pope John Paul I served for a mere 33 days in 1978, and President William Henry Harrison held the chief executive post for just 32 days before his death.

ADOLF AND RUDOLF DASSLER were very sneaky brothers, the creators of Adidas (1920) and Puma (1948) shoes, respectively.

AUTHOR! PSEUDONYM!

Name	*Pseudonym*
Kingsley Amis	Robert Markham
Hans Christian Andersen	Villiam Christian Walter
François-Marie Arouet	Voltaire
Isaac Asimov	Dr. A. Paul French
Louis Auchincloss	Andrew Lee
Robert Benchley	Guy Fawkes
Mildred Wirt Benson	Carolyn Keene
Marie Henri Beyle	Stendahl
Ambrose Bierce	Don Grile
Eric Arthur Blair	George Orwell
Charlotte Brontë	Lord Charles Wellesley
Charlotte Brontë	Marquis of Duoro
Emily Jane Brontë	Ellis Bell
Pearl Buck	John Sedges
William Burroughs	William Lee
Agatha Christie	Mary Westmacott
Samuel Langhorne Clemens	Mark Twain
Manfred B. Lee and Frederic Dannay	Ellery Queen
Charles Dickens	Boz
Charles L. Dodgson	Lewis Carroll
Cecily Isabel Fairfield	Rebecca West
Howard Fast	E. V. Cunningham
Edward Gorey	Hyacinthe Phypps
Dashiell Hammett	Peter Collinson
Carolyn Heilbrun	Amanda Cross
Josef Teodor Konrad Korzeniowski	Joseph Conrad

Name	*Pseudonym*
Evan Hunter	Ed McBain
Edna St. Vincent Millay	Nancy Boyd
Dorothy Parker	Constant Reader
Jean-Baptiste Poquelin	Molière
William Sydney Porter	O. Henry
Anne Rice	A. N. Roquelaure
William Saroyan	Sirak Goryan
Irving Tennenbaum	Irving Stone
Gore Vidal	Edgar Box

IT'S THE SAME OLD STORY . . .

Boys versus Girls in the Old Testament

Books Named After Boys

Joshua
Samuel (First Book)
Samuel (Second Book)
Ezra
Nehemiah
Tobit
Job
Sirach
Isaiah
Jeremiah
Baruch
Ezekiel
Daniel
Hosea
Joel
Amos
Obadiah
Jonah
Micah
Nahum
Habakkuk
Zephaniah
Haggai
Zechariah
Malachi

Books Named After Girls

Ruth
Judith
Esther

TOTALS: **BOYS: 25, GIRLS: 3**

PET NAMES

Animals We Know and Love

Name	*Animal*	*Owner*
Dinah	Cat	Alice in Wonderland
Garfield	Cat	Jim
Heathcliff	Cat	The Nutmeg Family
Mr. Bigglesworth	Cat	Dr. Evil of *Austin Powers*
Fred	Cockatoo	Baretta
Asta	Terrier	Nick and Nora Charles of *The Thin Man*
Astro	Mutt	The Jetsons
Brain the Wonder Dog	Mutt	Inspector Gadget
Brian	Mutt	The Griffins of *Family Guy*
Brandon	Golden Labrador	Punky Brewster
Daisy	Mutt	Dagwood Bumstead of *Blondie*
Dino	Dinosaur Dog	The Flintstones
Eddie	Jack Russell Terrier	Martin Crane of *Frasier*
Krypto	Super-Dog	Superboy

Lassie	Collie	Timmy Martin
Meathead	Bulldog	"Dirty Harry" Callahan
Mignon	Yorkshire Terrier	Lisa Douglas of *Green Acres*
Neil	St. Bernard	The Kerbys of *Topper*
Rin Tin Tin	German Shepherd	Corporal Rusty
Ruff	Airedale mix	Dennis the Menace
Snoopy	Beagle	Charlie Brown of *Peanuts*
Tiger	Sheepdog	The Brady Bunch
Tiger	Sheepdog	Patty Duke
Togo	Terrier	Nancy Drew
Triumph	Yugoslavian mountain dog	Conan O'Brien
Wishbone	Jack Russell	Joe Talbot
Woofer	Mutt	Winky Dink
Flipper	Dolphin	Sandy and Porter Ricks
Bimbo	Elephant	Corky of *Circus Boy*
Flicka	Horse	Ken McLaughlin
Silver	Horse	The Lone Ranger
Tornado	Horse	Zorro
Oscar	Lizard	Opie of *The Andy Griffith Show*

GREAT MINDS, RARELY THINKING ALIKE

Name	*Philosophy*
Anthisthenes (445–365 BCE)	Founder of Cynicism
Aristotle (384–322 BCE)	Offered roots of modern science and Western civilization nature
Saint Thomas Aquinas (1225–1274)	Provided Catholic Church much of its official dogma
Saint Augustine (354–430)	Founder of theology and cornerstone of the Christian Church
Martin Buber (1878–1965)	Dialogue between man and God is possible
August Comte (1798–1857)	Father of sociology; replaced the idea of God with the idea of mankind as a whole
René Descartes (1596–1650)	Father of the scientific method
John Dewey (1859–1952)	Pragmatist and educational theorist

Some Philosophies of Life . . . and Their Proponents

Best-known Work	*Quote*
No primary works survive	"I would rather go mad than feel pleasure!"
Organon	"Man is a political animal."
Summa Theologica	"Reason in man is rather like God in the world."
Confessions	"Will is to grace as the horse is to the rider."
I and Thou	"All journeys have secret destinations of which the traveler is unaware."
Introduction to Positive Philosophy	"Nothing at bottom is real except humanity."
Discourse on Method	"I think, therefore I am."
Democracy and Education	"Education is a social process. Education is growth. Education is, not a preparation for life; education is life itself."

Name	*Philosophy*
Friedrich Engels (1820–1895)	Cofounder of Marxism; originated philosophy of dialectical materialism
Epicurus (341–270 BCE)	Founder of Epicureanism
Georg Friedrich Wilhelm Hegel (1770–1831)	Thesis versus antithesis leads to synthesis
David Hume (1711–1776)	Argued against proofs of the existence of God
William James (1842–1910)	One of the founders of pragmatism; reality is what we make it
Immanuel Kant (1724–1804)	Founder of modern philosophy; the "thing-in-itself" cannot be known
Søren Kierkegaard (1813–1855)	Founder of existentialism; "truth is subjectivity"
Gottfried Wilhelm Von Leibniz (1646–1716)	Inventor of calculus; forefather of modern mathematical logic

Best-known Work	*Quote*
Dialectics of Nature	"The ruling ideas of each age have ever been the ideas of its ruling class."
Letter to Herodotus, *Letter to Pythocles*, *Letter to Menoeceus*	"The magnitude of pleasure reaches its limit in the removal of all pain."
Phenomenology of Spirit	"What is reasonable is real; that which is real is reasonable."
Enquiry Concerning Human Understanding	"Custom, then, is the great guide of human life."
The Will to Believe	"A thing is important if anyone think it important."
Critique of Pure Reason	"Though our knowledge begins with experience, it does not follow that it arises out of experience."
Either/Or	"Life can only be understood backwards; but it must be lived forwards."
Monadology	"I often say a great doctor kills more people than a great general."

Name	*Philosophy*
John Locke (1632–1704)	Ideas come from experience; none are innate
Niccolò Machiavelli (1469–1527)	Any act by a ruler to gain and hold power is permissible
Karl Marx (1818–1883)	It is human nature to transform nature
Friedrich Nietzsche (1844–1900)	God is dead
Blaise Pascal (1623–1662)	God cannot be known through reason, only through mystical understanding
Plato (c. 427–347 BCE)	Father of Western philosophy; recorded dialogues of Socrates
Jean-Paul Sartre (1905–1980)	One of the founders of existentialism; man is condemned to be free
Pyrrho of Elis (365–275 BCE)	Founder of Skepticism

Best-known Work	*Quote*
An Essay Concerning Human Understanding	"No man's knowledge here can go beyond his experience."
The Prince	"Among other evils which being unarmed brings you, it causes you to be despised."
Manifesto of the Communist Party	"Religion . . . is the opium of the people."
Thus Spake Zarathustra	"That which does not kill you makes you stronger."
Pensées	"Men blaspheme what they do not know."
Republic	"Democracy passes into despotism."
Existentialism and Human Emotions	"Hell is—other people."
No primary works survive	"Since nothing can be known, the only proper attitude is 'freedom from worry.'"

Name	*Philosophy*
Arthur Schopenhauer (1788–1860)	Believed the will is entirely real, but not free, nor does it have any ultimate purpose
Adam Smith (1723–1790)	Laissez-faire economic policy
Socrates (464–399 BCE)	Invented the practice of philosophical dialogue
Baruch Spinoza (1632–1677)	Mind and body are aspects of a single substance expressing God's plan
Alfred North Whitehead (1861–1947)	Integrated twentieth-century physics into a metaphysics of nature; "theology of organism
Ludwig Wittgenstein (1889–1951)	Philosophical problems are often caused by linguistic confusions
Zeno of Citium (336–264 BCE)	Founder of Stoicism

Best-known Work	*Quote*
The World as Will and Idea	"Every man takes the limit of his own field of vision for the limits of the world."
Wealth of Nations	"A monopoly granted either to an individual or to a trading company has the same effect as a secret in trades or manufactures."
No writings—Plato recorded his thoughts	"The unexamined life is not worth living."
Ethics	"Will and Intellect are one and the same thing."
Principia Mathematica (with Bertrand Russell)	"A culture is in its finest flower before it begins to to analyze itself."
Tractatus	"Whereof one cannot speak, thereof one must be silent."
No primary works survive	"Follow where reason leads."

WHO ROCKS

Rock & Roll Hall of Fame Members

CHARTER 1986 PERFORMER INDUCTEES

Chuck Berry * James Brown * Ray Charles * Sam Cooke * Fats Domino * Everly Brothers * Buddy Holly * Jerry Lee Lewis * Elvis Presley * Little Richard

1987

The Coasters * Eddie Cochran * Bo Diddley * Aretha Franklin * Marvin Gaye * Bill Haley * B. B. King * Clyde McPhatter * Ricky Nelson * Roy Orbison * Carl Perkins * Smokey Robinson * Big Joe Turner * Muddy Waters * Jackie Wilson

1988

The Beach Boys * The Beatles * The Drifters * Bob Dylan * The Supremes

1989

Dion * Otis Redding * The Rolling Stones * The Temptations * Stevie Wonder

1990

Hank Ballard * Bobby Darin * The Four Seasons * The Four Tops * The Kinks * The Platters * Simon and Garfunkel * The Who

1991

LaVern Baker * The Byrds * John Lee Hooker * The Impressions * Wilson Pickett * Jimmy Reed * Ike and Tina Turner

1992

Bobby "Blue" Bland * Booker T. and the MG's * Johnny Cash * The Isley Brothers * The Jimi Hendrix Experience * Sam and Dave * The Yardbirds

1993

Ruth Brown * Cream * Creedence Clearwater Revival * The Doors * Frankie Lymon and the Teenagers * Etta James * Van Morrison * Sly and the Family Stone

1994

The Animals * The Band * Duane Eddy * The Grateful Dead * Elton John * John Lennon * Bob Marley * Rod Stewart

1995

The Allman Brothers Band * Al Green * Janis Joplin * Led Zeppelin * Martha and the Vandellas * Neil Young * Frank Zappa

1996

David Bowie * Gladys Knight and the Pips * Jefferson Airplane * Little Willie John * Pink Floyd * The Shirelles * The Velvet Underground

1997

The (Young) Rascals * The Bee Gees * Buffalo Springfield * Crosby, Stills and Nash * The Jackson Five * Joni Mitchell * Parliament-Funkadelic

1998

The Eagles * Fleetwood Mac * The Mamas and the Papas * Lloyd Price * Santana * Gene Vincent

1999

Billy Joel * Curtis Mayfield * Paul McCartney * Del Shannon * Dusty Springfield * Bruce Springsteen * The Staple Singers

2000

Eric Clapton * Earth, Wind & Fire * Lovin' Spoonful * The Moonglows * Bonnie Raitt * James Taylor

2001

Aerosmith * Solomon Burke * The Flamingos * Michael Jackson * Queen * Paul Simon * Steely Dan * Ritchie Valens

2002

Isaac Hayes * Brenda Lee * Tom Petty and the Heartbreakers * Gene Pitney * Ramones * Talking Heads * Chet Atkins

2003

AC/DC * The Clash * Elvis Costello and the Attractions * The Police * The Righteous Brothers

2004

Jackson Browne * The Dells * George Harrison * Prince * Bob Seger * Traffic * ZZ Top

2005

Buddy Guy * The O'Jays * The Pretenders * Percy Sledge * U2

JAMES K. POLK was the first U.S. president to have a presidential photograph taken.

GROUP MYTHOLOGY

Fates (3)

The three daughters of Necessity: Life is woven by Clotho and measured by Lachesis, and the thread of life is cut by Atropos.

Winds (4)

Aeolus is the keeper of the winds; Boreas, the north wind; Eurus, the east wind; Notus, the south wind; Zephyrus, the west wind.

Muses (9)

The daughters of Zeus and Mnemosyne preside over arts and sciences: Calliope, epic poetry; Clio, history; Erato, lyric and love poetry; Euterpe, music; Melpomene, tragedy; Polyhymnia, sacred poetry; Terpsichore, choral dance and song; Thalia, comedy and bucolic poetry; and Urania, astronomy.

Furies (3)

The avenging spirits, daughters of Mother Earth: Alecto, unceasing in pursuit; Megaera, jealous; and Tisiphone, blood avenger.

LICENSE AND REGISTRATION, PLEASE . . .

We all know where the Three Wise Men were headed . . . but where were they from?

Balthazar was from Ethiopia and carried myrrh
Caspar came from Tarsus with frankincense
Melchior hailed from Arabia and brought gold

F. O. S.

Friends of Shakespeare . . . or, at Least, Who and What He Wrote About

Antony and Cleopatra: One of history's greatest couples, the Roman general Antony and the Egyptian queen Cleopatra. All Rome called her a sorceress as Antony gave away parts of the empire to Cleopatra and her children.

Coriolanus: Victorious yet prideful Roman general exiled from his native city; widely acknowledged to be the least sympathetic protagonist among Shakespeare's tragic figures.

Cymbeline: Wise and gracious king of Britain nearly destroyed by his wicked and conniving queen.

Hamlet: Shakespeare's most famous hero; a tragic prince who must choose between moral integrity and the need to avenge his father's murder.

Henry IV: The aging king of England joins with his wild adolescent son, Harry, to regain control of the country crumbling around him.

Henry V: England's rabble-rousing young prince becomes a brilliant young king and the revered ruler who conquers France.

Henry VI: A weak king who was never able to live up to the glories of his father, and who desired only to be an ordinary citizen.

Henry VIII: The larger-than-life king who changed England forever, bringing many wives and a new church to the palace.

Julius Caesar: Idolized Roman general and senator who falls prey to his public's idolization and belief in his own invincibility.

King John: Son of Henry II, though technically not next in line for the monarchy. Eventually he lost support and was killed by monks for stealing from their monasteries.

King Lear: The mad king whose demands on his daughters drove his family to rage and murder.

Macbeth: A murderous man determined to be king, whose power both rises and falls with the strength and fate of his wife.

Othello: Eloquent, respected, and powerful, this Moorish general is undone by jealousy and dies at his own hand.

Pericles: Like Job, a good man who conquers both men and fear, suffers many hardships, and is rewarded at last by reuniting with his own family.

Richard II: A regal, poetic young king attached much more to money and possessions than his people; eventually he is overthrown for his sins and assassinated.

Richard III: Deformed in body, twisted in mind, politically brilliant—and will stop at nothing, including murder, to be king.

Romeo and Juliet: Perhaps the most famous young couple in history, destined to die rather than live without each other.

Timon of Athens: Generous, wealthy man who later goes bankrupt, only to find he has no friends. He becomes a hermit, fortuitously finds a pot of gold, and uses it to have Athens destroyed.

Titus Andronicus: Heroic soldier and Shakespeare's bloodiest hero, he pursues revenge to the end (including cooking and serving his enemies), dying in the process.

Troilus and Cressida: Love goes bad between the prince of Troy, a valiant warrior, and a less-than-monogamous young woman, Cressida.

LADIES AND GENTLEMEN, THE BACH FAMILY!

Johann Sebastian Bach was the most famous musician of several generations of Bach musicians, starting with his great-grandfather, Veit Bach (1555–1619). Of J. S. Bach's twenty children, only three made anything of their musical training, none of them nearing the success of their prolific father.

When the family musicians became numerous and widely dispersed, they agreed to meet annually to discuss, compose, and play music together. This continued until the middle of the eighteenth century, with as many as 120 persons assembling, the fruits of which eventually formed a collection known as the Bach Archives. Here, a family tree on the most musical of the Bachs . . .

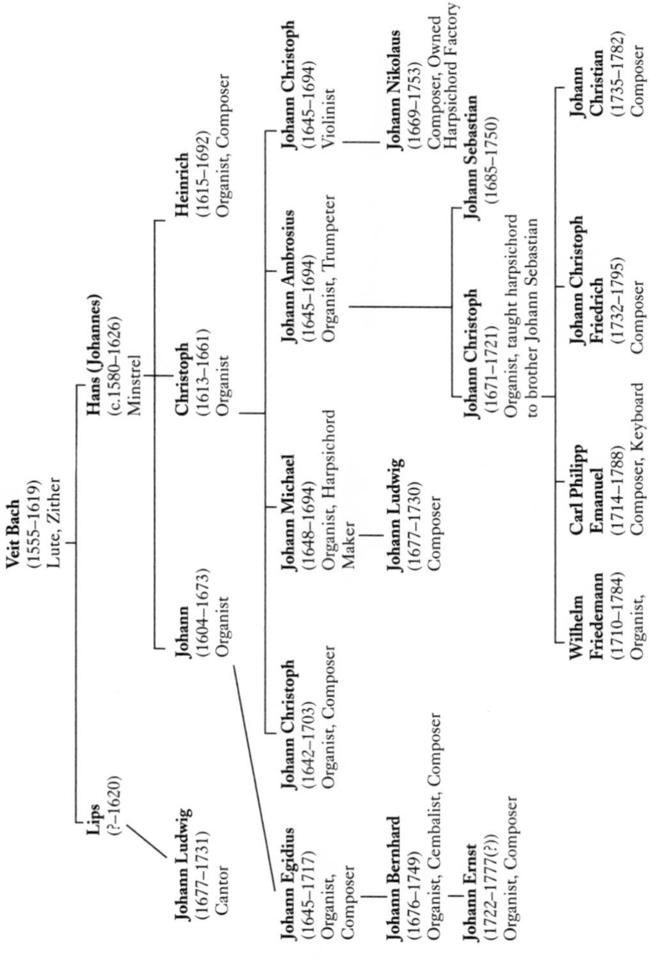
Veit Bach
(1555–1619)
Lute, Zither
Lips
(?–1620)
Hans (Johannes)
(c.1580–1626)
Minstrel
Johann Ludwig
(1677–1731)
Cantor
Johann
(1604–1673)
Organist
Christoph
(1613–1661)
Organist
Heinrich
(1615–1692)
Organist, Composer
Johann Egidius
(1645–1717)
Organist,
Composer
Johann Christoph
(1642–1703)
Organist, Composer
Johann Michael
(1648–1694)
Organist, Harpsichord
Maker
Johann Ambrosius
(1645–1694)
Organist, Trumpeter
Johann Christoph
(1645–1694)
Violinist
Johann Bernhard
(1676–1749)
Organist, Cembalist, Composer
Johann Ludwig
(1677–1730)
Composer
Johann Nikolaus
(1669–1753)
Composer, Owned
Harpsichord Factory
Johann Ernst
(1722–1777(?))
Organist, Composer
Johann Christoph
(1671–1721)
Organist, taught harpsichord
to brother Johann Sebastian
Johann Sebastian
(1685–1750)
Wilhelm
Friedemann
(1710–1784)
Organist,
Carl Philipp
Emanuel
(1714–1788)
Composer, Keyboard
Johann Christoph
Friedrich
(1732–1795)
Composer
Johann
Christian
(1735–1782)
Composer

BOND, JAMES BOND'S GIRLS

The Many Women in 007's Life

Lois Maxwell: Miss Moneypenny (1962–1985)
Caroline Bliss: Miss Moneypenny (1987–1989)
Samantha Bond: Miss Moneypenny (1995–present)
Ursula Andress: Honey Ryder: *Dr. No* (1962)
Daniela Bianchi: Tatiana Romanova:
From Russia with Love (1963)
Honor Blackman: Pussy Galore: *Goldfinger* (1964)
Shirley Eaton: Jill Masterson: *Goldfinger* (1964)
Claudine Auger: Domino Derval: *Thunderball* (1965)
Molly Peters: Patricia Fearing: *Thunderball* (1965)
Akiko Wakabayashi: Aki: *You Only Live Twice* (1967)
Diana Rigg: Tracy Di Vicenzo:
On Her Majesty's Secret Service (1969)
Jill St. John: Tiffany Case: *Diamonds Are Forever* (1971)
Jane Seymour: Solitaire: *Live and Let Die* (1973)
Britt Ekland: Mary Goodnight:
The Man with the Golden Gun (1974)
Barbara Bach: Anya Amasova: *The Spy Who Loved Me* (1977)
Lois Chiles: Dr. Holly Goodhead: *Moonraker* (1979)
Carole Bouquet: Melina Havelock: *For Your Eyes Only* (1981)
Maud Adams: Octopussy: *Octopussy* (1983)
Tanya Roberts: Stacey Sutton: *A View to a Kill* (1985)
Fiona Fullerton: Pola Ivanova: *A View to a Kill* (1985)
Maryam D'Abo: Kara Milvoy: *The Living Daylights* (1987)
Carey Lowell: Pam Bouvier: *Licence to Kill* (1989)
Talisa Suto: Lupe Lamora: *Licence to Kill* (1989)
Famke Janssen: Xenia Onatopp: *GoldenEye* (1995)
Teri Hatcher: Paris Carver: *Tomorrow Never Dies* (1997)
Michelle Yeoh: Wai Lin: *Tomorrow Never Dies* (1997)

Denise Richards: Dr. Christmas Jones:
The World Is Not Enough (1999)
Halle Berry: Jinx: *Die Another Day* (2002)
Dame Judi Dench: M (1995–present)

HOLLYWOOD'S MOST CELEBRATED

The Envelope, Please. . .
Oscar Winners with Four Wins

FOUR-TIME BEST ACTRESS WINNER

Katharine Hepburn
Morning Glory (1933)
Guess Who's Coming to Dinner (1967)
The Lion in Winter (1968)
On Golden Pond (1981)

FOUR-TIME BEST DIRECTOR WINNER

John Ford
The Informer (1935)
The Grapes of Wrath (1940)
How Green Was My Valley (1941)
The Quiet Man (1952)

SNOOPY'S SIBS

Before Charlie Brown, everyone's favorite beagle had another family at the Daisy Hill Puppy Farm . . .

Andy * Marbles * Rover * Olaf * Spike * Belle * Molly

Live from New York, It's THE ALBERT BROOKS SHOW *Or, As We All Know and Love It . . .* Saturday Night Live

ORIGINAL NOT READY FOR PRIME TIME PLAYERS
Dan Aykroyd (1975–1979)
John Belushi (1975–1979)
Chevy Chase (1975–1977)
Jane Curtin (1975–1980)
Garrett Morris (1975–1980)
Laraine Newman (1975–1980)
Gilda Radner (1975–1980)

NOT FEATURED
George Coe (1975)
Michael O'Donoghue (1975–1979)

CAST MEMBERS
Fred Armisen (2002–present)
Peter Aykroyd (1979–1980)
Morwenna Banks (1994–1995)
Jim Belushi (1983–1985)
Jim Breuer (1995–1998)
A. Whitney Brown (1985–1991)
Beth Cahill (1991–1992)
Dana Carvey (1986–1993)
Ellen Cleghorne (1991–1995)
Billy Crystal (1984–1985)
Joan Cusack (1985–1986)
Tom Davis (1977–1980)
Denny Dillon (1980–1981)
Jim Downey (1979–1980)
Robert Downey Jr. (1985–1986)
Brian Doyle-Murray (1979–1982)
Rachel Dratch (1999–present)
Robin Duke (1980–1984)
Nora Dunn (1985–1990)
Christine Ebersole (1981–1982)
Dean Edwards (2001–2003)
Chris Elliott (1994–1995)
Jimmy Fallon (1998–2004)
Siobhan Fallon (1991–1992)
Chris Farley (1990–1995)
Will Ferrell (1995–2002)
Tina Fey (2000–present)
Will Forte (2002–present)
Al Franken (1977–1980 and 1985–1995)

Janeane Garofalo (1994–1995)
Ana Gasteyer (1996–2002)
Gilbert Gottfried (1980–1981)
Mary Gross (1981–1985)
Christopher Guest (1984–1985)
Anthony Michael Hall (1985–1986)
Brad Hall (1982–1984)
Rich Hall (1984–1985)
Darrell Hammond (1995–present)
Phil Hartman (1986–1994)
Jan Hooks (1986–1991)
Yvonne Hudson (1980–1981)
Melanie Hutsell (1991–1994)
Victoria Jackson (1986–1992)
Chris Kattan (1995–2003)
Tim Kazurinsky (1980–1984)
Laura Kightlinger (1994–1995)
David Koechner (1995–1996)
Gary Kroeger (1982–1985)
Matthew Laurance (1980–1981)
Julia Louis-Dreyfus (1982–1985)
Jon Lovitz (1985–1990)
Norm MacDonald (1993–1998)
Gail Matthius (1980–1981)
Michael McKean (1993–1995)
Mark McKinney (1994–1997)
Tim Meadows (1990–2000)
Laurie Metcalf (1980–1981)
Seth Meyers (2001–present)
Dennis Miller (1985–1991)
Jerry Minor (2000–2001)
Finesse Mitchell (2003–present)
Jay Mohr (1993–1995)
Tracy Morgan (1996–2003)
Eddie Murphy (1980–1984)
Bill Murray (1976–1980)
Mike Myers (1988–1995)
Kevin Nealon (1986–1995)
Don Novello (1978–1980 and 1985–1986)
Cheri Oteri (1995–2000)
Chris Parnell (1998–present)
Joe Piscopo (1980–1984)
Amy Poehler (2001–present)
Randy Quaid (1985–1986)
Colin Quinn (1995–2000)
Jeff Richards (2001–2004)
Rob Riggle (2004–present)
Ann Risley (1980–1981)
Chris Rock (1990–1993)
Charles Rocket (1980–1981)

Tony Rosato (1980–1982)
Maya Rudolph (1999–present)
Adam Sandler (1990–1995)
Horatio Sanz (1998–present)
Tom Schiller (1979–1980)
Rob Schneider (1990–1994)
Molly Shannon (1994–2001)
Harry Shearer (1979–1980 and 1984–1985)
Martin Short (1984–1985)
Sarah Silverman (1993–1994)
Robert Smigel (1991–1993)
David Spade (1990–1996)
Pamela Stephenson (1984–1985)
Ben Stiller (1988–1989)
Julia Sweeney (1990–1994)
Terry Sweeney (1985–1986)
Kenan Thompson (2003–present)
Danitra Vance (1985–1986)
Dan Vitale (1985–1986)
Nancy Walls (1995–1996)
Damon Wayans (1985–1986)
Patrick Weathers (1980–1981)
Fred Wolf (1995–1997)
Alan Zweibel (1979–1980)

Over the years; Saturday night's favorite TV show has also been known as:

The Albert Brooks Show (working title)
NBC's Saturday Night (1975 original title)
SNL 25 (2000 new title)
SNL (1975)
Saturday Night Live '80 (1980 new title)

WALT DISNEY often washed his hands up to thirty times an hour—while Louis XIV hated washing so much it is believed that he bathed only three times in his entire life.

THE VALKYRIES

These beautiful young women scout battlefields to choose the bravest of the slain and bring them to Valhalla. The flickering light off their armor is the aurora borealis.

As they appear in traditional Norse mythology:

Brynhildr * Geriskögul * Göll * Göndul * Gudr * Gunn * Herfjoturr * Hildr * Hladgunnr * Hlokk * Hrist * Mist * Rathgrith * Rota * Sigrdrifa * Sigrún * Skagull * Skeggjald * Skuld * Svafa * Thrud

As they appear in Richard Wagner's *Der Ring des Nibelungen:*

Brunnhilde * Gerhilde * Grimgerde * Helmwige * Ortlinde * Rossweisse * Schwertleite * Siegrune * Waltraute

WHO'S ON TOP

Notable Women Given Honorary Degrees at Harvard Since Its Founding in 1636

Martha Graham (1966)
Georgia O'Keeffe (1973)
Beverly Sills (1974)
Barbara Jordan (1977)
Eudora Welty (1977)
Mother Teresa (1982)
Louise Nevelson (1985)
Toni Morrison (1989)
Ella Fitzgerald (1990)
Madeleine Albright (1997)
Gertrude B. Elion (1998)
Julia Kristeva (1999)
Ruth J. Simmons (2002)
Kathering Dunham (2002)
Margaret Atwood (2004)
Shirley M. Tilghman (2004)

MUSICAL GROUPS AND THEIR ORIGINAL MEMBERS

THE ANDREWS SISTERS
LaVerne Sofia, Maxene Angelyn, and Patty Marie Andrews

THE BAND
Robbie Robertson, Rick Danko, Richard Bell, Levon Helm, Garth Hudson, and Richard Manuel

THE BEATLES
George Harrison, John Lennon, Paul McCartney, and Stuart Sutcliffe

BUFFALO SPRINGFIELD
Richie Furay, Dewey Martin, Bruce Palmer, Stephen Stills, and Neil Young

THE DAVE CLARK FIVE
Dave Clark, Lenny Davidson, Rick Huxley, Denis Payton, and Mike Smith

DESTINY'S CHILD
Beyoncé Knowles, LaTavia Roberson, Kelendria (Kelly) Rowland, and LeToya Luckett

THE DIXIE CHICKS
Emily Erwin, Martie Erwin, Laura Lynch, and Robin Lynn Macy

THE DOORS
John Densmore, Robby Kreiger, Ray Manzarek, and Jim Morrison

THE FOUR TOPS
Levi Stubbs, Renaldo "Obie" Benson, Abdul "Duke" Fakir, and Lawrence Payton

THE GRATEFUL DEAD
Jerry Garcia, Bob Weir, Ron "Pigpen" McKernan, Phil Lesh, and Bill Kreutzmann

GUNS N' ROSES
Steve Adler, Mike "Duff" McKagan, Axl Rose, Slash, and Izzy Stradlin

THE INK SPOTS
Ivory "Deek" Watson, Jerry Daniels, Charles Fuqua, and Orville "Hoppy" Jones

THE JACKSON 5
Jackie, Marlon, Jermaine, Tito, and Michael Jackson

THE MCGUIRE SISTERS
Christine, Dorothy, and Phyllis McGuire

THE MONKEES
Micky Dolenz, Davy Jones, Mike Nesmith, and Peter Tork

THE OSMONDS
Alan, Wayne, Merrill, Jay, Donny, and Jimmy Osmond

THE ROLLING STONES
Mick Jagger, Brian Jones, Keith Richards, Charlie Watts, and Bill Wyman

THE SUPREMES
Florence Ballard, Diana Ross, and Mary Wilson

THE TEMPTATIONS
Eldridge Bryant, Melvin Franklin, Eddie Kendricks, Otis Williams, and Paul Williams

TRAFFIC
Dave Mason, Steve Winwood, Chris Wood, and Jim Capaldi

THE WHO
Roger Daltrey, John Entwhistle, Keith Moon, and Pete Townshend

FIFTH BEATLEMANIA!

Three people have been tagged the Fifth Beatle over the years: The first was original bass guitarist, Stu Sutcliffe, who played with the group until 1961; the second, manager Brian Epstein, so knighted by New York DJ Murray the K, and later, Beatles recording manager George Martin. Nowadays the term "fifth Beatle" is used to describe anyone who's missed out on success.

YANKEE INGENUITY?

In the nearly century-long history of the World Series, the New York Yankees have taken home baseball's greatest title twenty-six times. Second-place winners could hardly even be called runners-up: The St. Louis Cardinals have won nine times (the last time back in 1982).

REIGNS SUPREME

Supreme Court Justice William O. Douglas sat on the Big Bench for the longest time: thirty-six years, from 1939 to 1975.

Though Thomas Johnson served the shortest amount of time—he was sworn in August 6, 1792, and resigned on January 16, 1793—he is credited with writing the Supreme Court's very first decision.

Several religious denominations have been represented only once in the Supreme Court history:

John Rutlege (1790–1791 and 1795)	Church of England
Gabriel Duval (1811–1835)	French Protestant
Henry Baldwin (1830–1844)	Trinity Church
Noah H. Swayne (1862–1881)	Quaker
Joseph R. Lamar (1910–1916)	Church of Disciples
James C. McReynolds (1914–1941)	Disciples of Christ
William H. Rehnquist Jr. (1972–present)	Lutheran

And though several of the earlier justices came to America from Europe, two in the twentieth century were foreign-born: Justice David J. Brewer (1889–1910) was born in Asia Minor (in what is now Turkey) in 1837 to missionary parents who returned to the United States shortly after his birth; and Justice Felix Frankfurter (1939–1962) hailed from Vienna, Austria, and came to the United States in 1894 at the age of twelve.

EZRA J. WARNER invented the first can opener in 1858. Unfortunately, this was forty-five years *after* the invention of the tin can.

ADVERTISING ANIMALS

Axelrod	Flying "A" Service Stations dog
Bingo	Cracker Jack dog
Bucky Beaver	Ipana toothpaste
Charlie the Tuna	Starkist Tuna
The Counting Sheep	Serta Mattress
Dinky	Taco Bell chihuahua
Elsie the Cow	Borden's Milk
Farfel	Nestlé Quik dog
Frank and Louie	Budweiser frogs
The Gecko	Geico Insurance
Geoffrey	Toys "R" Us giraffe
Joe Camel	Camel cigarettes
Leo	MGM lion
Morris the Cat	Nine Lives Cat Food
Nipper and Lil' Nipper	RCA dogs
Polly	NBC peacock
Sharpie the Parrot	Gillette
Smokey the Bear	USDA Forest Service
Snoopy	Metropolitan Life (and *Peanuts*) beagle
Snuggle	Snuggle fabric softener bear
Sonny	Cocoa Puffs cuckoo bird
Spuds McKenzie	Bud Lite dog
Sugar Bear	Sugar Pops
Tige	Buster Brown Shoes dog
Tony the Tiger	Kellogg's Frosted Flakes
Toucan Sam	Froot Loops cereal bird
UBU Roi	UBU Productions (*Spin City*) dog
Willie	Kool penguin
Woodsy Owl	U.S. Forest Service

PRESIDENT RONALD REAGAN was older than JFK, Nixon, Ford, and Carter—four presidents who occupied the Oval Office before him.

FREE CONCERT!

Performers at Woodstock, August 15–17, 1969

AUGUST 15

Richie Havens
Country Joe McDonald
John Sebastian
Incredible String Band
Bert Sommer
Sweetwater
Tim Hardin
Ravi Shanker
Melanie
Arlo Guthrie
Joan Baez

AUGUST 16

Quill
Keef Hartley
Santana
Mountain
Canned Heat
Grateful Dead
Creedence Clearwater Revival
Janis Joplin
Sly and the Family Stone
The Who
Jefferson Airplane

AUGUST 17

Joe Cocker
Country Joe and the Fish
Ten Years After
The Band
Blood, Sweat and Tears
Johnny Winter
Crosby, Stills, Nash and Young
Paul Butterfield Blues Band
Sha Na Na
Jimi Hendrix

THE DISRUPTERS
CEOs Who've Changed the Face of Business

Janus Friis and Niklas Zennstrom, KaZaA: Inventors of the world's leading file-sharing software, which allows worldwide distribution of licensed works using peer-to-peer technology. They have also launched Skype, software that lets users place telephone calls over the Internet virtually free of charge and threatens to upend the telecommunications industry.

Bill Gates: Founder of the Microsoft Corporation, the largest software company in the world. Gates is also the richest man in the world.

Ray Kroc: Founder of McDonald's, the world's largest fast-food chain. Recognized that Americans don't dine—they eat and run.

Eli Pariser, MoveOn.org: This political activist changed the nature of the beast by creating this citizen mobilization Web site composed of three entities: helping members elect candidates; education and avocation on national issues; and education of voters on positions, records, views, and qualifications of political candidates.

Jim Press, Toyota: The only American on the Japanese company's board of directors is bringing the United States into the future with the much-vaunted hybrid automobile, the Prius, the gas-electric vehicle voted 2004 Car of the Year by *Motor Trend* magazine.

Mike Ramsay and Jim Barton, TiVo: In conceiving TiVo, these two men transformed the way people watch television. This popular DVR (digital video recorder) has enjoyed one of the most rapid adoption rates ever in consumer electronics.

James Sinegal, CostCo: The founder of the members-only warehouse—who got his chops at Price Club—is selling to both consumers and small and medium retailers. Revenues and popularity are making even Wal-Mart take notice.

Martha Stewart: America's most trusted style guru, famous for her Emmy Award–winning *Martha Stewart Living* television show, many books, and magazines.

Sam Walton: Founder of Wal-Mart, the largest U.S. retailer, featuring low prices and one-stop shopping. Walton changed the face of retailing today, contributing to the downsizing of family-run Mom and Pop stores throughout the country.

After selling his steel business, ANDREW CARNEGIE pursued his lifelong dream: trying to give away all his money. Interest on his money grew so fast, however, that he never managed to fulfill his dream, though when he died in 1919, Carnegie had donated 90 percent of his $125 million, primarily through the Carnegie Endowment for International Peace and the Carnegie Corporation, the latter a philanthropic trust to fund libraries; aid colleges, universities, and technical schools; and promote scientific research.

GREAT SONGS ABOUT EPHEMERAL SOMEONES

Who put the bomp in the bomp ba bomp ba bomp,
Who put the ram in the rama lama ding-dong?
Who Put the Bomp in the Bomp Ba Bomp Ba Bomp?

Who threw the overalls in Mrs. Murphy's chowder?
Nobody spoke, so she shouted all the louder
It's an Irish trick that's true,
I can lick the mick who threw
The overalls in Mrs. Murphy's chowder.
Who Threw the Overalls in Mrs. Murphy's Chowder?

Who's that knocking at my door?
Barnacle Bill the Sailor

Who's sorry now?
Who's sorry now?
Who's heart is aching for breaking each vow?
Who's Sorry Now?

Who's afraid of the big bad wolf?
Who's Afraid of the Big Bad Wolf? (based on Johann Sebastian Strauss's "Champagne Song" from *Die Fledermaus*)

HERMANN RORSCHACH'S SECRET

Actually, there are ten secrets. The inkblots the general public typically sees as examples of Rorschach inkblots are just that: examples. The real inkblots used in Rorschach's psychological testing are copyrighted and kept under tight wraps, so that testees have no prior knowledge.

MUTUALLY INCLUSIVE

The only person to be featured in both the "Got milk?" mustache ads and "What becomes a legend most?" Blackglama mink ads:

Lauren Bacall

The only character to be part of both the *Sesame Street* and *The Muppet Show* casts:

Kermit

The only men to sign both the Declaration of Independence and the Constitution:

Roger Sherman of Connecticut
Benjamin Franklin of Pennsylvania
Robert Morris of Pennsylvania
George Clymer of Pennsylvania
James Wilson of Pennsylvania
George Read of Delaware

MAN, OH, MAN

The Seven Ages of Man, According to the Bard, William Shakespeare

The infant
The whining schoolboy
The lover
The soldier
The justice
The lean and slipper'd pantaloon
Second childishness and mere oblivion

WHO'S YOUR GOD?

Top 10 Organized World Religions by Population Ranking

Religion	*Members*
Christianity	2.1 billion
Islam	1.3 billion
Hinduism	900 million
Buddhism	376 million
Sikhism	23 million
Judaism	14 million
Baha'i Faith	7 million
Confucianism	5.3 million
Jainism	4.2 million
Shinto	4 million

SCAREDY CATS

A Few Phobias of the Famous

Katharine Hepburn	Trichopathophobia (fear of dirty hair)
Madonna	Brontophobia (fear of thunder)
Queen Christina of Sweden	Acarophobia (fear of fleas)
Elizabeth I	Anthophobia (fear of roses)
Sid Caesar	Tonsurphobia (fear of haircuts)
Sigmund Freud	Siderodromophobia (fear of train travel)
Augustus Caesar	Ailurophobia (fear of cats)

CHRISTOPHER PLUMMER on Julie Andrews: "Working with her is like being hit over the head with a Valentine's card."

BASIC ORGANIZATION OF THE ROMAN LEGION

Contubernium	Tent party	8
Ten contubernium	One century (basic unit of imperial legion)	80
Two centuries	One maniple (administrative/training)	160
Six centuries	One cohort (main battlefield/tactical unit)	480*
Ten cohorts	One legion	5,120*

*The first cohort, made up of the elite troups, consisted of five double centuries, 800 men, rather than the 480 in each of the remaining cohorts.

Ranking of Soldiers

Legatus	Commander of a legion who had six tribunes as subordinates; these officers were generally drawn from the senatorial class
Tribune	Generally a young aristocrat
Centurion	Lowest commissioned rank
Cornicularius	Top sergeant
Optio	Sergeant
Signifer	Standard-bearer
Librarius legionus	Divisional clerk, a sort of cushy clerical job
Legionary	Backbone of the Roman army
Auxiliary	Drawn from Roman colonies or provinces

WHO'S UP THERE?

In his 1972 book *The UFO Experience: A Scientific Study*, Dr. J. Allen Hynek, an astronomy professor at Ohio State University, devised one of the most famous contributions to UFOlogy, the Hynek Classification System—a way to categorize or group UFO sightings as either "distant sightings" or "close encounters."

Close Encounter of the First Kind (CEI)	A UFO is within 500 feet of the experiencer
Close Encounter of the Second Kind (CEII)	A UFO leaves marks on the ground, may cause burns or paralysis to humans, scares animals, interferes with car engines or TV and radio reception
Close Encounter of the Third Kind (CEIII)	A CEI or CEII that has visible occupants
Close Encounter of the Fourth Kind (CEIV)	Abduction
Close Encounter of the Fifth Kind (CEV)	Communication between human and alien

PRESIDENT JOHN TYLER (1841–1845) has earned the title Father of Our Country in more ways than one. He had more offspring than any other Oval Office resident—fifteen children—though it took him two wives and several years after The Job to do it.

POP TOPS

Top Pop Music Artists of Each Decade of the Twentieth Century and Their Most Popular Song

1900–1909	Billy Murray	"Take Me Out to the Ball Game"
1910–1919	Henry Burr	"In the Shade of the Old Apple Tree"
1920–1929	Paul Whiteman	"It's Only a Paper Moon"
1930–1939	Bing Crosby	"Out of Nowhere"
1940–1949	Bing Crosby	"White Christmas"
1950–1959	Elvis Presley	"Hound Dog"
1960–1969	The Beatles	"She Loves You"
1970–1979	The Bee Gees	"Stayin' Alive"
1980–1989	Michael Jackson	"Thriller"
1990–1999	Mariah Carey	"Sweetheart"

Bing Crosby had the most Top 40 tunes in the twentieth century with ninety-three songs. They ranged from "Out of Nowhere" in 1931 (number 1 for three weeks, number 7 for the year) to "True Love" in 1956 (number 27 for the year). His biggest hit was "White Christmas," which spent eleven weeks at number 1 in 1945—though the film by the same name was not released until 1954.

HERE COMES THE GROOM

At an estimated 1,400 pounds, Jon Brower Minnoch outweighed his 110-pound wife, Jeanette, by at least 1,290 pounds, the world's greatest recorded marital weight difference. They had two children before Mr. Minnoch died at age forty-two in 1983.

FOLKS WHO ARE SO BIG THEY HAVE THEIR OWN FESTIVAL

Festival	*Honoring*
Abraham Lincoln National Rail-Splitting Festival	Celebrates young lawyer's efforts to bring railroad through town
Annie Oakley Days	Famous Wild West sharpshooter
Bill Williams Rendezvous	Rough-and-ready frontier scout
Chester Greenwood Day	Inventor of the earmuffs
Daniel Boone Festival	Archetypal American
Defeat of Jesse James	Notorious Wild West outlaw
Hemingway Days	Writer, drinker, reveler

From the "Isn't America Great?" Files—

Locale	*Events*
Lincoln, Illinois	Junior and senior rail-splitting competitions, flea market, frontier display
Greenville, Ohio	Shooting contests, balloon rallies, old-time melodramas, parade
Williams, Arizona	Roping, parade, black powder shoot, cowboy barbecue, arts and crafts, music and dancing
Farmington, Maine	Old-time vaudeville shows, invention displays, parade
Barbourville, Kentucky	Pioneer village, pioneer long-rifle shootout, square dancing, pioneer crafts, quilt show, parade
Northfield, Minnesota	Reenactment of raid, rodeo, parade, outdoor art and food fair
Key West, Florida	Storytelling competitions, armwrestling contests, "Papa" Hemingway lookalike show, Caribbean street festival

Festival	*Honoring*
The Jeanie Auditions	Mrs. Stephen Foster "with the light brown hair"
Jim Butler Days	Lost a burro, found a silver mine
Lum 'n' Abner Days	Slice-of-Arkansas-life radio stars
Stonewall Jackson Heritage Jubilee	Revered Confederate General
Tom Sawyer Days	Fictional all-American boy

. . . And a Couple of Very Special Groups

Cowboy Poetry Reading	Sensitive, sentimental cowpokes
National Hobo Convention	Newspaper gag turned nostalgic fete

Locale	*Events*
White Springs, Florida	Contest for composer Stephen Foster's wife ("I Dream of Jeanie with the Light Brown Hair"), vocal competition, folk art exhibit and ball
Tonopah, Nevada	Miner competitions, chili cook-offs, barbecue, catfish fry, stock-car races, Old West entertainment, parade
Mena, Arkansas	Children's beauty pageant, quilt show, basketball camp, arts fair
Weston, West Virginia	Mountain crafts and music, traditional dancing, Civil War reenactment, food booths, arts fair
Hannibal, Missouri	Whitewashing competition, jumping frog contest, tomboy games, fireworks, tours of Hannibal, Missouri, mud volleyball tournament
Elko, Nevada	Poetry readings, seminars in songwriting, rawhide braiding, silversmithing, and western cooking
Britt, Iowa	Carnivals, talent show, hobo parade, serving of mulligan stew

WHO'S WHO

Since the first *Who's Who* (8,602 people were listed) in 1899, Marquis, the publishing house, has built a biographical fiefdom that includes:

Who's Who in America
Who Was Who in America
Who's Who in 20th Century America
Who's Who in the World
Who's Who on the Web

Who's Who in the East
Who's Who in the Midwest
Who's Who in the South and Southwest
Who's Who in the West

Who's Who in American Art
Who's Who in American Education
Who's Who in American Law
Who's Who in American Politics
Who's Who of American Women
Who's Who in Finance and Business
Who's Who in Medicine and Healthcare
Who's Who in Science and Engineering

Moby-Dick author HERMAN MELVILLE died as a patent clerk, so out of fashion and forgotten that his *New York Times* obituary repeatedly referred to him as Henry Melville.

NOTES FROM THE SYMPHONY

Who's in Charge at America's Biggest, or, Different Notes for Different Folks

TWO SYMPHONIES, ONE MUSICAL DIRECTOR

Michael Tilson Thomas serves as musical director of the New World Symphony and San Francisco Symphony

JoAnn Falletta is at both the Buffalo Philharmonic and the Virginia Symphony

WOMEN IN CHARGE (IN ADDITION TO MS. FALLETTA, ABOVE)

Anne Manson at the Kansas City Symphony
Kate Tamarkin at the Monterey Symphony
Gisèle Ben-Dor at the Santa Barbara Symphony Orchestra

MUSICAL DIRECTORS WHOSE NAMES HAVE AN UMLAUT

Paavo Järvi of the Cincinnati Symphony Orchestra
Franz Welser-Möst at the Cleveland Orchestra
Neeme Järvi at the Detroit Symphony Orchestra
Gürer Aykal at the El Paso Symphony Orchestra
Osmo Vänskä at the Minnesota Orchestra

THE KFC 3

Colonel Harlan Sanders shared his secret recipe with only two others—his wife, Claudia, and Jack C. Massey, head of the syndicate that bought the corporation in 1964. Others learn only how to cook the chicken, not what's in the secret recipe.

BEST JOURNALISTS OF THE 20TH CENTURY*

So Good They Were Voted the Top 100—More Than Once

Edward R. Murrow	Battle of Britain, CBS radio (1940) Report of the Liberation of Buchenwald, CBS radio (1945)
Edward R. Murrow and Fred Friendly	Investigation of Senator Joseph McCarthy, CBS (1954)
Edward R. Murrow, David Lowe, and Fred Friendly	*Harvest of Shame*, documentary, CBS television (1960)
Tom Wolfe	*The Electric Kool-Aid Acid Test*, book (1968) *The Kandy-Kolored Tangerine-Flake Streamline Baby*, collected articles (1965) *The Right Stuff*, book (1979)
James Baldwin	*The Fire Next Time*, book (1963) "Letter from the South: Nobody Knows My Name," *The Partisan Review* (1959)
W. E. B. Du Bois	*The Souls of Black Folk*, collected articles (1903) Columns on race while editor of *The Crisis* (1910–1934)
John Hersey	"Hiroshima," *The New Yorker* (1946) *Here to Stay*, collected articles (1963)

Murray Kempton	*America Comes of Middle Age: Columns 1950–1962*, collected articles (1963) *Part of Our Time: Some Ruins and Monuments of the Thirties*, book (1955)
Norman Mailer	*The Armies of the Night*, book (1968) *The Executioner's Song*, book (1979)
Bob Woodward and Carl Bernstein	Investigation of the Watergate break-in, *The Washington Post* (1972) *All the President's Men*, book (1979)

*According to a New York University Journalism Department panel vote.

HISPANIC AMERICAN NOBEL PRIZE WINNERS

Severo Ochoa, biochemist, for work on the synthesis of RNA (1959)

Luis Walter Alvarez, physicist, inventor of radio distance and direction indicator (1968)

Mario Molina, chemist, for work in atmospheric chemistry, particularly his study of the ozone layer (1995)

GORE VIDAL on RONALD REAGAN: "A triumph of the embalmer's art."

HINDU CLASSES

Hindi are separated into castes, a hereditary social class system stratified according to ritual purity.

Brahmins: the highest, or priestly, class
Kshatriyas: royal and warrior class
Vaisyas: mercantile and professional class
Sudras: working class

General Hierarchal Hindu Caste System

1. Persons of holy descent
2. Landowners and administrators
3. Priests
4. Craftsmen
5. Agricultural tenants and laborers
6. Herders
7. Despised persons, or untouchables

The Hindu caste system is thought to have begun around 1500 BCE with the invasion of India by the Aryans, and though "untouchability" has been officially abolished, it is still somewhat in practice.

"Who could ask for anything more?" Not the GERSHWIN BROTHERS, apparently. They used the phrase in three of their songs:

"I Got Rhythm," from 1930's *Girl Crazy*
"I'm About to Be a Mother," from *Of Thee I Sing* in 1931
"Nice Work If You Can Get It," from the 1937 movie *A Damsel in Distress*

TITLE-ISTS: HOW TO READ THE SHEEPSKIN

AB	artium baccalaureus (bachelor of arts)
AM	artium magister (master of arts)
BA	bachelor of arts
BD	bachelor of divinity
BS	bachelor of science
DB	divinitatis baccalaureus (bachelor of divinity)
DD	dovonitatis doctor (doctor of divinity)
DDS	doctor of dental surgery
DO	doctor of osteopathy
DVM	doctor of veterinary medicine
JD	juris doctor (doctor of law)
LHD	litterarum humaniorum doctor (doctor of humanities)
LittD	litterarum doctor (doctor of letters)
LLB	legum baccalaureus (bachelor of laws)
MA	master of arts
MD	medicinae doctor (doctor of medicine)
MLitt	master of literature
MS	master of science
PhB	philosophiae baccalaureus (bachelor of philosophy)
PhD	philosophiae doctor (doctor of philosophy)
PhG	graduate in pharmacy
PsyD	doctor of psychology
RN	registered nurse
SB	scientus baccalaureus (bachelor of science)
SM	scientus magister (master of science)
STB	sacrae theologiae baccalaureus (bachelor of sacred theology)

TONY CURTIS on Marilyn Monroe: "It's like kissing Hitler."

FANNY BRICE on Esther Williams: "Wet she's a star. Dry she ain't."

BRITISH ROYAL LINE OF SUCCESSION*

1. HRH Prince Charles, the Prince of Wales (1948)
2. HRH Prince William of Wales, eldest son of Prince Charles (1982)
3. HRH Prince Henry of Wales, younger son of Prince Charles (1984)
4. HRH Prince Andrew, the Duke of York, second son of Queen Elizabeth II (1960)
5. HRH Princess Beatrice of York, elder daughter of Prince Andrew (1988)
6. HRH Princess Eugenie of York, younger daughter of Prince Andrew (1990)
7. HRH Prince Edward, the Earl of Wessex, youngest son of Queen Elizabeth II (1964)
8. Lady Louise Alice Elizabeth Mary Mountbatten Windsor, daughter of Prince Edward, the Earl of Wessex (2003)
9. HRH Princess Anne, the Princess Royal, only daughter of Queen Elizabeth II (1950)
10. Peter Phillips, son of Princess Anne (1977)
11. Zara Phillips, daughter of Princess Anne (1981)
12. David Armstrong-Jones, Viscount Linley, son of Princess Margaret (1961)
13. The Honorable Charles Patrick Inigo Armstrong-Jones, son of David, Viscount Linley (1999)
14. Margarita Elizabeth Rose Alleyne Armstrong-Jones, daughter of David, Viscount Linley (2002)
15. Lady Sarah Chatto, daughter of Princess Margaret (1964)

*As of 2004.

AKA

Prince Charles of Great Britain holds all of these titles (and more):

Prince of Wales
Duke of Cornwall
Duke of Rothesay
Earl of Carrick
Baron of Renfrew
Lord of the Isles
Prince and Great Steward of Scotland
Earl of Chester

ORDER OF BRITISH PEERAGE

1. Duke and duchess
2. Marquess and marchioness
3. Earl and countess
4. Viscount and viscountess
5. Baron and baroness

VICTORIA CLAFLIN WOODHULL (1838–1927) was the first woman nominated for the U.S. presidency. In 1872, the Equal Rights Party picked Woodhull to represent them for her early advocacy of an eight-hour workday, graduated income tax, social welfare programs, and profit sharing. Her candidacy was supported by laborers, female suffragists, spiritualists, and communists. The Equal Rights Party also nominated Frederick Douglass, the first African American to run for vice president in U.S. history.

FORTUNE 500 TOP MINORITY EMPLOYERS

Company	*Percentage of Minority Employees*
Union Bank of California	55.6
McDonald's	53.1
PNM Resources	48.5
Sempra Energy	48.0
Denny's	47.4
Southern California Edison	44.9
Fannie Mae	44.7
U.S. Postal Service	36.4
Freddie Mac	33.5
PepsiCo	27.3

PROFILES IN COURAGE, written by then-Senator John F. Kennedy, is the only Pulitzer Prize–winning biography by a U.S. president. It is the story of eight other U.S. senators and how they manifested what JFK considered the most admirable of human virtues, and what Ernest Hemingway called "grace under pressure"—courage.

John Quincy Adams (1767–1848)
Daniel Webster (1782–1852)
Thomas Hart Benton (1782–1858)
Sam Houston (1793–1863)
Lucius Quintas Cincinnatus Lamar (1825–1893)
Edmund G. Ross (1826–1907)
George Norris (1861–1944)
Robert A. Taft (1889–1953)

VERY, VERY MARRIED

"She cried, and the judge wiped her tears with my checkbook."

—TOMMY MANVILLE

King Mongut of Siam (1804–1868), depicted in *The King and I*	9,000 wives and concubines
King Solomon of the Old Testament (970–928 BCE)	700 wives
Brigham Young, Mormon of Salt Lake City (1801–1877)	27 wives
Calamity Jane (*née* Martha Cannary) of the United States (1852–1903)	12 husbands
Tommy Manville of the United States (1894–1967)	11 wives
Pancho Villa of Mexico (1878–1923)	9 wives
Artie Shaw of the United States (1910–2005)	8 wives
Mickey Rooney of the United States (1920–)	8 wives
Elizabeth Taylor of Hollywood (1932–)	7 husbands

IT'S THEIR PARTY

Presidents Elected Without Any Party Affiliation

George Washington (1789)
John Quincy Adams (1824)

Author WINSTON CHURCHILL (1871–1947) wrote several bestsellers—mostly historical fiction of the American south—at the turn of the century. His most outstanding success, *Richard Carvel*, sold 2 million copies upon publication in 1899 . . . in a country of only 72 million people. This particular Winston Churchill did not go on to become the prime minister of England, though he met and occasionally communicated with that British statesman. In fact, because the 10 Downing Street resident's works reached the bookshelves later, his book jackets always read Winston S. Churchill.

MERRY CHRISTMAS!

Born on December 25

Sir Isaac Newton, scientist (1642)
Conrad Hilton, hotelier (1887)
Dame Rebecca West, novelist (1892)
Cab Calloway, jazz singer (1907)
Anwar Sadat, statesman (1918)
Little Richard, singer (1932)
Annie Lennox, singer (1954)

LOGGING ON @ THE START

Some surprising folks were the Internet's earliest computer geeks . . .

- The first world leader to send an e-mail was Queen Elizabeth in 1976.
- Jimmy Carter and Walter Mondale used e-mail to plan their campaign events, also in 1976.
- Novelist William Gibson coined the word *cyberspace* in 1984.

WHO DIED AND MADE YOU QUEEN?

The Reigns of Ten Allegedly Gay Monarchs

William II of England 1087–1100
Richard I of England 1189–1199
Edward II of England 1307–1327
John II of France 1350–1364
James III of Scotland 1469–1488
Henri III of France 1574–1589
James I of England (James VI of Scotland) 1603–1625
Louis XIII of France 1610–1643
Mary II of England, Scotland, and Ireland 1689–1694
Anne of Great Britain and Ireland 1702–1714

CURIOUS, THE AMISH . . .

They May Not	*But They May*
Have a phone at home, as it might promote gossip	Use a phone outside the home
Own a car	Hitch a ride from an "English" friend
Have electricity in their home	Use 12-volt batteries to run appliances
Swear an oath in court	Make an "affirmation of truth" in court

WARD MCALLISTER was the coiner of several high-society words and *bon mots*, including *snob* and *bon vivant*; he also named Mrs. Astor's closest pals The Four Hundred.

BETTER LIVING THROUGH SCIENCE

Some Scientists and Their Steps Through Time

Hippocrates (c. 460–377 BCE)
Father of medicine

Euclid (c. 300 BCE)
Geometry

Nicholas Copernicus (1473–1543)
Sun is center of the solar system

Galileo Galilei (1564–1642)
Father of astronomy and physics

Robert Hooke (1635–1703)
Invented the quadrant,
Gregorian telescope,
and microscope

Sir Isaac Newton (1642–1727)
Law of Gravity

Charles Darwin (1809–1882)
Theory of evolution

Jean Foucault (1819–1868)
Foucault's pendulum

Gregor Johann Mendel (1822–1884)
Modern genetics

Louis Pasteur (1822–1895)
Immunization and
pasteurization

Wilhelm Conrad Roentgen (1845–1923)
X-ray machine

Sigmund Freud (1856–1939)
Father of psychoanalysis

Leo Baekeland (1863–1944)
Bakelite, the first popular plastic

Marie Curie (1867–1934) and Pierre Curie (1859–1906)
Radiology

Wilbur Wright (1867–1912) and Orville Wright (1871–1948)
Heavier-than-air flight

Ernst Rutherford (1871–1937)
Father of nuclear physics

Albert Einstein (1879–1955)
Theory of relativity

Edwin Hubble (1889–1953)
Universe is expanding

Robert J. Oppenheimer (1904–1967)
Father of the Atomic Bomb

Philo T. Farnsworth (1906–1971)
Vacuum tube television

Rachel Carson (1907–1964)
Environmental movement

Jonas Salk (1914–1995)
Polio vaccine

James Dewey Watson (1928–) and Francis Crick (1916–2004)
DNA double helix

WOMEN OF MANNERS

Modern-Day Grandes Dames of Etiquette

EMILY POST

"Manners are a sensitive awareness of the feelings of others. If you have that awareness, you have good manners, no matter what fork you use."

AMY VANDERBILT

"Good manners have much to do with the emotions. To make them ring true, one must feel them, not merely exhibit them."

LETITIA BALDRIDGE

"When you put your foot in your mouth, eject it—quickly!"

MISS MANNERS (NÉE JUDITH MARTIN)

"We are all born charming, fresh and spontaneous, and must be civilized before we are fit to participate in society."

W. E. B. DU BOIS was the first African American to receive a Ph.D. from Harvard, in 1895.

BIG DAY

On these dates, someone famous died . . . and someone famous was born.

Date	*Died*	*Born*
May 19, 1795	Biographer James Boswell	Philanthropist Johns Hopkins
July 4, 1826	Presidents John Adams and Thomas Jefferson	Songwriter Stephen Foster
October 15, 1917	Spy Mata Hari	Historian Arthur Schlesinger Jr.
May 23, 1934	Bank robbers Clyde Barrow and Bonnie Parker	Inventor Robert Moog
January 5, 1945	Seer Edgar Cayce	Musician Stephen Stills
November 21, 1945	Humorist Robert Benchley	Actress Goldie Hawn

. . . and these folks were born on the very same day.

James Cagney and Erle Stanley Gardner, born July 17, 1899
Marlon Brando and Doris Day, born April 3, 1924
Eartha Kitt and Roger Vadim, born January 26, 1928
Luciano Pavarotti and Joan Rivers, born October 12, 1935
Princess Margaret and Janis Joplin, born January 19, 1943
George Foreman and Linda Lovelace, born January 10, 1949

KILLING MACHINES

Name/Handle	*When and Where*	*Number of Victims*
David Berkowitz/ "Son of Sam"	1970s New York	Killed 6; wounded 7
Kenneth Bianchi and Angelo Buono/ "The Hillside Stranglers"	1977–1978 United States	9 convictions
Ted Bundy	1970s United States	28 confessions
Jeffrey Dahmer	1980s Milwaukee	16
Albert DeSalvo	1962–1964	13 women
Albert Fish	1919–1928 United States	8–15
John Wayne Gacy/ "The Killer Clown"	1978–1981 Chicago	30+
Pedro Lopez/ "Monster of the Andes"	1970s Peru, Ecuador, and Colombia	300+
Robert Pickton	1990s Vancouver	30+
Aileen Wournos	1989–1990	6 convictions

Some of History's Most Gruesome Serial Killers

M.O.	*Weird Fact*
44-caliber killer; stalked lovers' lanes	Took his orders from a dog
Sodomize, strangle, leave on a hillside	Posed as policemen
Charming psychopath raped college girls	Urban legend has Deborah Harry as an escaped victim
Cannibalism and necrophilia of young boys	Impaled animal heads on sticks as a child
Sex and murder	"Measuring Man" told women he was from a modeling agency
Rape, torture, cannibalize, and try new children recipes; Hannibal Lector model	Liked to be beaten with a nail-studded paddle
Torture, rape, and murder young men; hid remains under the floorboards	Had his photo taken with First Lady Rosalyn Carter
Rape and murder of young girls, often three a week	Had "tea parties" with little girls after he killed them
Killed prostitutes and kept body parts in freezers	Chopped body parts into pig feed
Lesbian who worked as prostitute and killed men	Played in the movie *Monster* by one of Hollywood's most beautiful actresses, Charlize Theron

DAY JOBS

Famous People, Ordinary Work

Jeffrey Archer (author): Deckchair attendant
Hannah Arendt (political philosopher): First Princeton woman professor
Jon Bon Jovi (rock star): Christmas ornament maker
Dominick Dunne (writer, investigative journalist): Producer
T. S. Eliot (poet): Bank clerk
Benjamin Franklin (scientist and statesman): Promoter
Washington Irving (author): Diplomat
James Fenimore Cooper (author): Gentleman farmer
Ralph Waldo Emerson (poet): Unitarian minister
Friedrich Engels (coauthor of *The Communist Manifesto*): Textile manufacturer
Che Guevara (Cuban revolutionary): Doctor
Nathaniel Hawthorne (author): Surveyor
Adolf Hitler (Leader of the Third Reich): House painter
Mick Jagger (rock star): Mental hospital porter
Cyndi Lauper (pop star): Dog kennel cleaner
Malcolm X (Nation of Islam leader): Burglar
Herman Melville (author): Customs inspector
Gertrude Stein (author): Medical student
Wallace Stevens (poet): Insurance executive
Rod Stewart (rock star): Gravedigger
Harriet Beecher Stowe (abolitionist): Housewife
Hunter S. Thompson (author): Sportswriter
Henry David Thoreau (naturalist): Pencil maker
Lionel Trilling (literary critic): College professor
Mark Twain (author): Riverboat pilot
William Carlos Williams (poet): Pediatrician

SEBASTIAN CLOVER became the youngest person ever to sail the Atlantic single-handedly in 2003. He was just fifteen years old and was racing against his father.

SOME YOUNG MEN RAISED AS YOUNG LADIES

Boy	*Girlish Past*	*Macho Future*
Robert Peary (1856–1920)	"Bertie" wore frills and sunbonnets	North Pole explorer
Douglas MacArthur (1880–1964)	Skirts and curls	General
Ernest Hemingway (1899–1961)	Frilly dresses	Great American novelist
Peter Paul Rubens (1577–1640)	Lacy underwear, gowns, and wigs	Flemish artist
Rainier Maria Rilke (1875–1926)	"Sophie," ages one to six	Austrian poet
Oscar Wilde (1854–1900)	Dresses of blue velvet	Irish playwright
Thomas Wolfe (1900–1938)	Long, hand-curled hair	U.S. novelist
Alexander Woollcott (1887–1943)	Dressed as "Alexandra"	U.S. essayist

HONORARY CITIZENS OF THE UNITED STATES

In the history of the United States, there have been only six:

Sir Winston Churchill (1874–1965)	British Prime Minister during World War II; citizenship conferred 1963
Raoul Wallenberg (1912–?)	Swedish diplomat and Holocaust hero; citizenship conferred 1981
William Penn (1644–1718) and Hannah Penn (1671–1727)	Founder of Pennsylvania and his second wife, who administered the Province of Pennsylvania after his death; citizenship conferred 1984
Mother Teresa, *née* Agnes Gonxha Bojaxhim (1910–1997)	Macedonian nun and civil rights advocate; citizenship conferred 1996
The Marquis de Lafayette (1757–1834)	The French supporter of the American Revolution was made an honorary citizen many times, but not of the United States as a whole until 2002

GEORGE W. BUSH was the president elected with the most popular votes: 62,028,772 (yet with only 50.8 % of the popular vote) in 2004.

LESSER-KNOWN GOLDWYNISMS

"Every director bites the hand that lays the golden egg."
"I had a monumental idea last night but I didn't like it."
"Tell me, how did you love my picture?"
"I never liked you, and I always will."
"It's more than magnificent—it's mediocre."
"It's spreading like wildflowers."
"This makes me so sore it gets my dandruff up."
"Color television! Bah, I won't believe it until I see it in black and white."
"If I could drop dead right now, I'd be the happiest man alive."
"A bachelor's life is no life for a single man."

THE WORLD'S MOST PROLIFIC PAINTER

Created an estimated
13,500 paintings and designs,
100,000 prints and engravings,
34,000 book illustrations and
300 sculptures and ceramics

and quite possibly possessed the longest artist's name:

Pablo Diego José Francisco de Paula Juan Nepomuceno Crispin Crispiniano los Remedios Cipriano de la Santisima Trinidad Ruiz Blasco y Picasso Lopez
AKA
Pablo Picasso

AT LAST . . .
Famous Folks' Final Words

"Why not, why not, why not. Yeah."	—Timothy Leary
"Stand away, fellow, from my diagram."	—Archimedes
"Damn it....Don't you dare ask God to help me out."	—Joan Crawford
"It is very beautiful over there."	—Thomas Edison
"I'm losin'."	—Frank Sinatra
"All my possessions for a moment of time."	—Elizabeth I
"This is the last of earth! I am content."	—John Quincy Adams
"Get my swan costume ready."	—Anna Pavlova
"Moose. Indian."	—Henry David Thoreau
"I'll finally get to see Marilyn."	—Joe DiMaggio
"Crito, I owe a cock to Asclepius; will you remember to pay the debt?"	—Socrates
"I've never felt better."	—Douglas Fairbanks Jr.
"Go on, get out. Last words are for fools who haven't said enough."	—Karl Marx
"Please put out the lights."	—Theodore Roosevelt
"I have a terrific headache."	—Franklin Delano Roosevelt
"Curtain! Fast music! Lights! Ready for the last finale! Great! The show looks good. The show looks good."	—Florenz Ziegfeld
"I am not the least afraid to die."	—Charles Darwin
"We've caught them napping!"	—General Custer, at Little Big Horn

"I go to seek the great Perhaps."	—Francois Rabelais
"Well, I must arrange my pillows for another weary night! When will this end?"	—Washington Irving
"Thou, too, Brutus, my son!"	—Julius Caesar
"Let us go in; the fog is rising."	—Emily Dickinson

WOMEN'S WORK

Leading Occupations Held Predominantly by Females

Job	*Median Weekly Earnings ($)*
1. Secretary	591
2. Registered nurse	887
3. Nursing, home health care	372
4. Cashier	315
5. Customer service representative	503
6. Office supervisor	609
7. Retail supervisor	496
8. Bookkeeping, auditing clerk	512
9. Receptionist	446
10. Accountant	756
11. Retail sales	382
12. Maid	317
13. High school teacher	824
14. Waitress	318
15. Teaching assistant	344
16. Office clerk	502
17. Financial representative	823
18. Preschool teacher	493
19. Cook	317

DISEASES NAMED AFTER PEOPLE

Creutzfeld-Jakob Disease: Encephalopathic disease commonly known as "Mad Cow" (1920)

Legionnaire's Disease: Infection that leads to pneumonia, named for the initial two hundred Philadelphia conventioneers who contracted it (1976)

Down Syndrome: Condition in which a person has three of chromosome 21 instead of two (1866)

Cushing's Disease: Hormonal condition brought on by high levels of cortisol (1932)

Hodgkin's disease: Cancer of the lymphatic system whose cause remains unknown, but may be related to Epstein-Barr virus, which causes mononucleosis (1832)

Marfan Syndrome: Connective tissue problems found in very tall people (1896)

Munchausen Syndrome: Hypochondriac's obsessive need to procure attention (1951)

Munchausen-by-Proxy: Condition in which, to garner attention, a parent causes a child to become sick (1977)

Parkinson's Disease: Neurological condition affecting the central nervous system (1817)

Raynaud's Disease: Vessel contraction in the fingers and toes, causing numbness and tingling (1862)

Reyes Syndrome: Children's organ disorder resulting from chicken pox or flu (1963)

Tay-Sachs Disease: Rare inherited disease causing slow destruction of the central nervous system (1969)

Tourette's Syndrome: Neurological disorder manifesting itself in tics (1885)

FAMOUSLY ILLEGITIMATE

Sarah Bernhardt, actress
Pope Clement VII
Leonardo da Vinci, artist
Frederick Douglass, abolitionist
Josephine de Beauharnais, Napoleon's wife
Alexander Hamilton, U.S. secretary of the treasury
Jenny Lind, singer
Marilyn Monroe, actress
Richard Wagner, composer
William the Conquerer, first Norman ruler

DID YOU WHISTLE FOR ME?

A majority of the thirty most popular pet names are also people names, according to the ASPCA. Some of the top monikers are:

Max * Sam * Kitty * Molly * Buddy * Brandy * Ginger * Misty * Missy * Jake * Samantha * Muffin * Maggie * Charlie * Rocky * Rusty * Buster

Some are named for other types of animals:

Bear * Tiger

And some are actually named for what most pets think they in fact are—royalty:

Lady * Princess

AMERICA'S BEST PRESIDENTIAL NICKNAMES

George Washington: Sword of the Revolution
John Adams: Old Sink or Swim
Thomas Jefferson: Pen of the Revolution
James Monroe: Last of the Cocked Hats
John Quincy Adams: Accidental President
Andrew Jackson: King Andrew the First
Martin Van Buren: Petticoat Pet
W. H. Harrison: Old Granny
Millard Fillmore: American Louis Philippe
Franklin Pierce: Purse
James Buchanan: Ten-Cent Jimmy
Abraham Lincoln: Illinois Baboon
Andrew Johnson: Sir Veto
Ulysses S. Grant: Useless Grant
Rutherford B. Hayes: His Fraudulency
Chester A. Arthur: Dude President
Grover Cleveland: Buffalo Hangman
Benjamin Harrison: Grandfather's Hat
William McKinley: Wobbly Willie
Theodore Roosevelt: Great White Chief
Woodrow Wilson: Coiner of Weasel Words
Herbert Hoover: Hermit Author of Palo Alto
Franklin D. Roosevelt: Sphinx
Harry S. Truman: Haberdasher Harry

MARY FAIRFAX SOMERVILLE was the first woman to have a scientific paper presented before the British Royal Society, in 1826.

OVAL OFFICE ODDITIES

Clothes Hog

Chester Allan Arthur owned more than 80 pairs of trousers.

The "Hanging Sheriff"

Grover Cleveland was the only president to personally hang anyone. "Buffalo's Hangman" threw the noose and sprung the trap on two convicted criminals while sheriff of Erie County, New York.

In the Raw

John Quincy Adams insisted on swimming in the nude.

STD

JFK had a nearly perpetual case of chlamydia.

Backroom Politics

Warren G. Harding gambled White House china in a poker game—and lost the china. The lucky winner took it home.

. . . And the Most Expensive Non–White House Race

Michael R. Bloomberg ran the most costly nonpresidential campaign in U.S. history. In his 1998 New York City mayoral campaign, he spent $73 million.

WHO APPEARS MOST OFTEN IN CROSSWORD PUZZLES?

Prophets
In order of popularity:

Major
Isaiah * Jeremiah * Ezekiel * Daniel

Minor
Hosea * Obadiah * Nahum * Haggai * Joel * Jonah * Habakkuk * Zechariah * Amos * Micah * Zephaniah * Malachi

Canadian Jurists
In word-length order, alphabetically:
Caron * Jette * Armour * Davies * Mulock * Stuart * Doherty * Lacoste * Fournier * Haultain * Newcombe * Richards * Robinson * Haliburton * Fitzpatrick

Hunting Dogs
In word-length order, alphabetically:
Alan * Brach * Rache * Ratch * Alaund * Basset * Hunter * Kennet * Lucern * Racche * Saluki * Seizer * Setter * Slough * Courser * Dropper * Harrier * Pointer * Striker

Playwrights from Around the World
Chambers (Australia) * Maeterlinck (Belgium) * Rose (Canada) * Tammsaare (Estonia) * Ilg (Switzerland) * Evans (Wales) * Chikamatsu (Japan) * Gamboa (Mexico) * Silva (Portugal) * Blaga (Romania)

U.S. POETS LAUREATE

Joseph Auslander (1937–1941)
Allen Tate (1943–1944)
Robert Penn Warren (1944–1945)
Louise Bogan (1945–1946)
Karl Shapiro (1946–1947)
Robert Lowell (1947–1948)
Leonie Adams (1948–1949)
Elizabeth Bishop (1949–1950)
Conrad Aiken (1950–1952)
William Carlos Williams (1952)
Randall Jarrell (1956–1958)
Robert Frost (1958–1959)
Richard Eberhart (1959–1961)
Louis Untermeyer (1961–1963)
Howard Nemerov (1963–1964)
Reed Whittemore (1964–1965)
Stephen Spender (1965–1966)
James Dickey (1966–1968)
William Jay Smith (1968–1970)
William Stafford (1970–1971)
Josephine Jacobsen (1971–1973)
Daniel Hoffman (1973–1974)
Stanley Kunitz (1974–1976)
Robert Hayden (1976–1978)
William Meredith (1978–1980)
Maxine Kumin (1981–1982)
Anthony Hecht (1982–1984)
Robert Fitzgerald and Reed Whittemore (1984–1985)
Gwendolyn Brooks (1985–1986)
Robert Penn Warren (1986–1987)
Richard Wilbur (1987–1988)
Howard Nemerov (1988–1990)
Mark Strand (1990–1991)
Joseph Brodsky (1991–1992)
Mona Van Duyn (1992–1993)
Rita Dove (1993–1995)
Robert Hass (1995–1997)
Robert Pinsky (1997–2000)
Stanley Kunitz (2000–2001)
Billy Collins (2001–2003)
Louise Gluck (2003–2004)
Ted Kooser (2004–)

U.S. poets laureate are appointed for one year, but eligible for reappointment.

PRESIDENTS ELECTED WITHOUT A MAJORITY

Year	*Winner*
1824	John Quincy Adams (D-R)
1844	James K. Polk (D)
1848	Zachary Taylor (W)
1856	James Buchanan (D)
1860	Abraham Lincoln (R)
1876	Rutherford B. Hayes (R)
1880	James A. Garfield (R)
1884	Grover Cleveland (D)
1888	Benjamin Harrison (R)
1892	Grover Cleveland (D)
1912	Woodrow Wilson (D)
1916	Woodrow Wilson (D)
1948	Harry S. Truman (D)
1960	John F. Kennedy (D)
1968	Richard M. Nixon (D)
1992	William J. Clinton (D)
1996	William J. Clinton (D)
2000	George W. Bush (R)

D-R: Democratic-Republican; D: Democrat; W: Whig; R: Republican

Though Americans are now quite used to close presidential elections and a long wait for results, the 1876 vote between Rutherford B. Hayes and Samuel B. Tilden still holds first

Fifteen of Our Commanders in Chief—
And Three of Them Twice

Opponent	*Percentage of Electoral Votes*	*Percentage of Popular Votes*
Andrew Jackson	32.2	30.9
Henry Clay	61.8	49.5
Lewis Cass	56.2	47.3
John C. Fremont	58.8	45.3
John C. Breckinridge	59.4	39.8
Samuel J. Tilden	50.1	47.9
Winfield S. Hancock	58.0	48.3
James G. Blaine	54.6	48.5
Grover Cleveland	58.1	47.8
Benjamin Harrison	62.4	46.0
Theodore Roosevelt	81.9	41.8
Charles E. Hughes	52.2	49.2
Thomas E. Dewey	57.1	49.6
Richard M. Nixon	56.4	49.7
Hubert H. Humphrey	56.0	43.4
George H. Bush	68.8	43.0
Robert J. Dole	70.5	49.2
Albert A. Gore	50.4	47.9

place in America's collective political breath-holding record books. Hayes was announced the winner of the November 7 race on March 2, 1877—three days before his inauguration.

ROBERT URICH starred in fifteen television series, more than any other actor to date:

Bob & Carol & Ted & Alice (1973)
S.W.A.T. (1975–76)
Soap (1977–81)
Tabitha (1977–78)
Vega$ (1978–81)
Gavilan (1982)
Spenser: For Hire (1985–88)
American Dreamer (1990–91)
National Geographic Explorer (1991–94)
Crossroads (1992)
It Had to Be You (1993)
The Lazarus Man (1996)
Vital Signs (1997)
Boatworks (1997)
Love Boat: The Next Wave (1998–99)

A POPULAR, TRENDY COCKTAIL
The Dr. Kevorkian

1 oz Amaretto
1 oz Southern Comfort whiskey
1 oz Jack Daniels whiskey
1 oz gin
1 oz vodka
8 oz orange juice
Serve over ice.

WHO BOLTED?

The Confederate States of America

State	*Date Seceded from Union*	*Date Readmitted to Union*
1. South Carolina	Dec. 20, 1860	July 9, 1868
2. Mississippi	Jan. 9, 1861	Feb. 23, 1870
3. Florida	Jan. 10, 1861	June 25, 1868
4. Alabama	Jan. 11, 1861	July 13, 1868
5. Georgia	Jan. 19, 1861	July 15, 1870
6. Louisiana	Jan. 26, 1861	July 9, 1868
7. Texas	March 2, 1861	March 30, 1870
8. Virginia	April 17, 1861	Jan. 26, 1870
9. Arkansas	May 6, 1861	June 22, 1868
10. North Carolina	May 20, 1861	July 4, 1868
11. Tennessee	June 8, 1861	July 24, 1866

SNL HOSTS WITH THE MOST

Celebs Who Keep Coming Back for More

Steve Martin (13 appearances) * John Goodman (12 appearances) * Alec Baldwin (11 appearances) * Buck Henry (10 appearances) * Chevy Chase (8 appearances)

SNL'S LONGEST-LASTING CAST MEMBERS

Al Franken (11 years) * Tim Meadows (10 years) * Darrell Hammond (10 years) * Kevin Nealon (9 years) * Phil Hartman (8 years)

THE SIX WIVES OF HENRY VIII

Queen	*Birth–Death*	*Wifely Years*	*Fate*
Catherine of Aragon	1485–1536	1509–1533	Divorced
Anne Boleyn	1507?–1536	1533–1536	Executed
Jane Seymour	1509?–1537	1536–1537	Died
Anne of Cleves	1515–1557	January–July 1540	Divorced
Katherine Howard	?–1542	1540–1542	Executed
Katherine Parr	1512–1548	1543–1547	Widowed

ALGONQUIN ROUND TABLE

1919–1943

Dorothy Parker * Alexander Woollcott * Heyward Broun * Robert Benchley * Robert Sherwood * George S. Kaufman * Franklin P. Adams * Marc Connelly * Harold Ross * Harpo Marx * Russel Crouse

MUSICIANS WHO DIED IN PLANE CRASHES

Glenn Miller (1944) * Big Bopper (1959) * Buddy Holly (1959) * Richie Valens (1959) * Patsy Cline (1963) * Otis Redding (1967) * Jim Croce (1973) * Ricky Nelson (1985) * Stevie Ray Vaughn (1990) * John Denver (1997)